# BEST OF THE EAST*

---

KNOW WELL & PRACTICE WELL
TO SPREAD "PIETY** & PEACE"

* 'Sanatan Dharma' **Devotion

K. CHANDRAMOULI

INDIA • SINGAPORE • MALAYSIA

ISBN  979-8-88833-692-2

# BRIEF VIEW OF THE TWO CONCEPTS OF

## Pt. MADAN MOHAN MALAVIYA
### AIMED AT BOTH  BEST OF THE WEST & EAST

WEST FOR **'PROGRESS & PROSPERITY'**
IN OUR POOR COUNTRY

EAST FOR
**BRIGHT GLOW TO CONTROL FIVE SENSORS**

TRAIN FROM **MODERN EDUCATION**
& GAIN FROM **GOLDEN ADVICE**

# 'BEST OF THE WEST' CONCEPT

ATTAIN PROGRESS & PROSPERITY IN MANY WAYS*
(*Limit to Science & Technology)
PROGRESS FROM
**DOWN IN THE SEA TO UP IN THE SKY**
**PROSPERITY HANKERS FOR CRAVE & CRAZE****
**FALLING DOWN IN ROUGH TRACKS IN PRICKY WAYS**
(**Mind Ruffled By Five Sensory Organs -
Eye, Ear, Nose,Tongue and Touch)

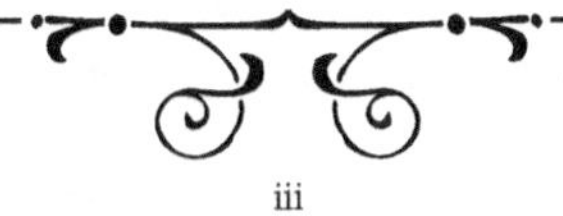

# 'BEST OF THE EAST' CONCEPT*

(*Sanatan Dharma)

## GOOD THOUGHTS, SENSIBLE DISCUSSIONS & BEST RELATIONS

Spiritual Principles, Right Path, Proper Acts

Healthy, Beneficial, Harmonious Life

LEAD TO **"PIETY & PEACE "** ALL AROUND.


## DRASTIC  CHANGES  IN 75 YRS  AFTER  Pt. MALAVIYA

## WHAT HAS  CHANGED & HOW TO RESTORE NOW?

Our country has changed considerably compared to 1916-1946, when Pt. Malaviya established BHU and lived for 30 years. Modern Education from West and in our own country resulted in tremendous improvemnet in **'Progress and Prosperity'**. The second objective of **"Best of the East"** or **Sanatan Dharma**, in the past 75 years after his demise, was struck in the worst, the most pitiable deterioration and neglect. Frequent disturbances, strikes etc became common and increased over the years, in BHU. Suggestions made by two separate, expert panels did not continue for long. There is not much to talk about **'Piety & Peace'** or **"Devoutness & Peace"**.

As if the Sanskrit name and subject (Sanatan Dharma) are not universal, many Units used "Value Education"--also not fully followed. Pt. Malaviya had given enough encouragement and facilities (apart from basic Education) for Extra Curricular Activities like sports, swimming, Boy Scout, Cultural Activities etc. Presently, not many Universities consider even Value Education  as Extra Curricular Activities for good life mentioned in Dharma earlier like - Love / Peace at Home, Friend in Group, Unity in Community, Progress In State, and Patriotism in Country!!

In short, Pt. Malaviya's **Best of the East Concept** has not only to be revived correctly in BHU, but also spread all over the country and become an  'Extra Curricular Activity' in all Universities.  Just lectures on 'Sanatan Dharma' as a part of study will not be useful; they may not become interesting to students, may be forgotten in short time, may not be followed in practice. Efforts should be made to convert the important Sanatan phrases into a practical exercise for a group of students. The **practical exercise** can be used in Social Service in nearby villages. **Social Service** when based on Sanatan Dharma will strike deep in the memory of students. Practical Experience will do a good work, students will understand its importance and its good feelings for a life-long time. They will initiate their young family in similar lines.

# CONTENTS

# INTRODUCTION

The name of the present subject as "**Best of the East**" appears delusive till it is explained that it is the moderate '**spiritual**' part of the two Objectives of the Banaras Hindu University. Another part of the Objective was named as the "**Best of the West**", which is likely to  overflow with the best; and the overflow may also hit hard, like roaring waves of sea, to badly damage the voyage or reverse the path away from the goal. '**Best of the East**' corrects the journey in many ways--with a well laid path, a bright light to show the clean path, an indicator (guide) towards the goal, a break to control the speed of run and like a firm mind to take the smooth drive to the correct and safe destination.

Apart from the Gurukul system of education, BHU was the first of the country's 'Teaching University' out of the total six non-teaching Universities then; also it was the first University to have such two clear Objectives! A few torturing calamities are mentioned here--high poverty stuck with big unemployment since 1750s, frequent famines and plague attacks, **British** Government not fulfilling promises for better education, the country's literacy falling down to very poor level at 5%, no interest by Govt to improve industries in India, the Govt sending more Indentured Labourers **across the sea to other countries** instead of increasing local employment.

Pt. Malaviya had come to the conclusion that '**Education**' at different levels was the only solace for gradually coming out of various problems in the Country. In order to hasten the issue, he had thought of establishing a separate, private University. Request to Govt for approval continued, in different phases, from 1904 to1916. Hard work and details are dealt in a separate booklet. Finalising of the two **Objectives** of the University was also important. Pt. Malaviya set the first Objective as the **"Best of the West"** in order to get the benefits of 'Education' in **Science and Technology** and the development in industries from Western countries, who had advanced in Science & Technolgy and  Industrial Revolution. Thus **"Best of the West"** definitely was to lead our country towards the bright light of 'Education' and Industries to bring in '**Progress**' and '**Prosperity**'.

Pt. Malaviya as a strong spiritualist from his birth, could also see that the back-bone of the British country was in **War and Trade.** Their natural tendency was to crave more for **Progress** and **Prosperity**,  with frequent war and trade with weaker countries. This type of **Progress** and **Prosperity,** without spirituality would lead to uncontrolled bad ways of living with others (considered as different from them). Our country was strong in war (as was necessary with Ravana) and also in spirituality, both from the time of Ramayan. This was symbolised in many *Shlokas* (verses) like "*Sarve Bhavantu Sukhinah, Sarve Santu Niraamaya....*"( may every one live happily, in peace...as it was in Rama Rajya)-- People lived a life based on Dharma, which always directed towards unity, calmness, **'Peace and Piety'** in all ways. Piety means **devotedness** or '*Shraddha* in Dharma', which says that one has to be-- peaceful at home, friendly in groups, helpful in communities, unity in state, patriotic in the country, and finally considering **Ekatva** with one and all the beings in the universe. Thus, Dharma does not teach different religious ways of prayers or poojas to the Supreme, but guides all in the peaceful ways of living for self and all others.

While the Gurukul system concentrated more on

spiritual living and spreading 'Piety and Peace', Pt. Malaviya wanted both the objectives-- 'Progress and Prosperity' to strengthen our poor country and also 'Piety and Peace' to live in peace with one and all. His idea was to balance both the Objectives to guide the Education in our Country. The Objectives were maintained well till Pt. Malaviya lived (1946) and a few years later; because the staff and students considered him as an honourable saint, whose presence, talks and directives had to be respected in all ways.

Today almost all the educational institutions (Schools, Colleges and Universities) are keen that the students should be trained to acquire mainly "**Progress and Prosperity**" in future. Apart from Science and Technology, today there are many institutions to give education and training in innumerable other courses/subjects. After the courses, the students look for good earnings that consequently lead to 'Progress and Prosperity' of their families. What is trained to students in modern days may not be from the 'Best of the West' only, but from any other country in the world. Thus, most of the well trained students are likely to enjoy the 'Progress and Prosperity' in inumerable ways of earning. In the process, they would copy, enjoy and possibly get used to the different customs and cultures of other countries. Since the five sensors (Eye, Ear, Nose, Tongue and Touch) are tempted by countless attractions, their habits and customs get changed, their known culture gets replaced by new cultures/habits and their noble tradition and heritage are cut short to the end by throwing it off as a useless or **dirty** fruit!!

Simple example is about the wide changes between the friendly matches of the past and the commercialisation of sports or cultural activities. A sixer in earlier cricket was appreciated by clapping even by the bowler or opposite captain also - showing their true sportsmanship. In today's commercial cricket, a wicket is treated by the bowler and the entire fielding team to shout harshly, make worst-awkward faces to mock at the poor batsman, and other worse gestures to show that they are enemies!! Similar is the worst example of our recent cinema scenes of 'lust'.

These bad changes will take place, if the various institutions (in our country) do not train students properly in the "Best of the East" policy and then take pride about their goal towards "Progress and Prosperity". Attention to values and strict discipline in the institution or outside are needed. In other words, what is needed in the "Best of the East" policy today is to build character (do's and dont's) that is learnt from Dharma, to maintain or improve our culture; and  not to fall prey to "Angreziyat" or outside glamours, but to spread the "Heritage" from ages with our pride.....etc.

However it is difficult to understand the second Objective **"Best of the East" to create "Piety and Peace". It is a** difficult and a long explanation. Hence this major second Objective is not covered in the Introduction, but given in detail in the text. A few small examples are given here to get a glimpse at **"How Animosity & Intolerance"** grow up when 'Best of East' policy with Dharma is not used----one of the latest examples is given below--

The rules/principles of the University are some times set aside due to a problem and then even a small argument leads to destructive activities. It is like forcing a Guru to accept their demands a) against the principles of Gurukul, b) for non-vegetarian food or else...; c) protests to keep Library open till 12 midnight for both boys and girls (because girls have equal rights) etc.   One group demands for it and another shouts against it. This internal fight soon expands to rowdyism and breaking of chairs, instruments, glass windows and ....the big loss would be seen by the third party (the University). This type of disturbance in any University may be related to the

<u>absence</u> of "Best of the East" policy and the absence of proper coachings to the students to follow Dharma! Also it shows that mere coaching of certain subjects by lectures would not be useful; each Institution has to frame its own 'Practical Performances' or Social Activities on different problems of the day. Groups have to go to the problem area, meet the group of persons facing the problem and find a solution or help them by contributions etc. Such practical ventures give many advantages to students--they mingle with persons in trouble; understand the problems; try for possible solutions; get more advice; make up their mind to help the poor/problematic persons; feel good for helping/solving a problem---etc. This is the way to learn and work on many aspects or essence of Sanatan Dharma.

The chapter starts with the worst condition of our countrymen in many aspects, during the rule of British-Indian Government and how Pt. Malaviya was keen on establishing a private university. Today's problems can be tackled by using the principles of Sanatan Dharma, by the students in various educational institutions. There are a number of books on the subject of 'Sanatan Dharma' and examples of six/seven books have been given in this booklet. Sringeri Jagadguru Sri Sri Bharati Teertha Swamiji has given the meanings and in a number of speeches has explained the way of 'What should be done?'. Example--"Whether you are a great scholar or a rich person, you have to follow Dharma, and be away from Adharma; because these two are the reasons for hapiness or sorrow.

Person doing Adharma may initially get the win; but later will suffer...". This type of explanations are clear for elders and  students also. Meanings given in many other books are shown in the **Appendix**. Any one interested may make use of them for some more reading and explanations.

There are many purposes for writing on this subject.  It can be used in many ways--

1) to use the subject as a part of the Orientation Course for students, at the time of their admission to the College/University.

2) to familiarise the importance of Sanatan Dharma to the new teachers/professors, so that they can properly guide the students for practical applications of social service.

3) to have a Conference of  the Senior Government Officials of  Education in all States and also the heads of Universities in all the states, so  that a) they can discuss, correct, change and think of implementing this policy in any better ways, b) they help all students, in any institution, to know about the essence of mutual help, unity, patriotism, culture, heritage etc.,

4) to ensure that the students now and elders later in our country understand and follow the importance of Dharma--the right way of living life (at home, in community, in the country--from love at home, mutual help in society---- to Patriotism in the country).

5) Finally to get the advantages of - 'Best of the East Policy' - by controling the misuse in a high level of - 'Progress and  Prosperity'- (without spirituality) would lead to uncontrolled bad ways of living with others, they would copy, enjoy and get used to the different customs and cultures of other countries, their habits and customs get changed, their known culture gets replaced by new cultures/habits and their noble tradition and heritage are cut short to the end by throwing it off as a useless or dirty fruit.

# Chapter - 1

# FALL OF OUR GREAT COUNTRY 

Our country was at its best in many respects for many centuries upto the 10-11th century AD. Foreign invaders, whose major and central aims were to loot the riches of the country, gradually captured and ruled part or full of some kingdoms of the country. We now come directly to the British trade and the British rule in our country. There were some positive points of the trade and British Rule from 1600 AD till our independence in 1947. But the negative points that badly hurt the common men (in high population) are not forgotten even now. Vareity of problems like large scale industrial unemployment, agriculture hit by famines, poverty, plague, bad sanitation, lack of education, ignorance to find a safe path etc-- these problems virtually picturise the long Rule of the Britishers. That constant pain and bad suffering in darkness of those centuries cover up, ignore the few good points of their Rule.

(**Note**-Pt. Madan Mohan Malaviya's speeches etc are made use of for the **Introduction,** along with a few additional paras, before changing over to the subject of "**Best of the East**"- the important subject of this book)

The British Naval groups (whose main interest or objective was to Trade), even ransacked few naval boats/vessels of their neighbouring countries. For this great performance, the Queen had awarded Knighthood to the leader! British traders initially begged and got the permission from Queen, to stay in India for trade. British Royal Charter of

**1600** approved the East India Company. The Company set in motion a process that ultimately resulted in the subjugation of India under East India Company (till 1857) directly and under the British Government rule (from 1858).

British Rulers of India, for a long period, badly hit our normal living and culture. They forced different views and actions, flavoured by dictatorship. Our spiritual thoughts and education activities were badly affected when our Gurukul education activities were badly affected by the British compulsion to follow 'Angreziyat' (known as Macaulay's Kiss and Kick). People's literature, culture, customs, heritage were twisted and affected badly. (Even the Sanskrit University in Banaras was closed by British). Major part of the atmosphere in the country became **musty** (smelling sour or tasting stale) like that of a dirty stenchy pond. Freedom was choked harder by the day in their reign of silent terror! Poverty was spread every where, by drastically degrading our (handicraft) items compared to their (machine made) items of 'Industrial Revolution' (1760-1820). Indian Manufacturers/ artists/traders who were famous in trade for centuries suddenly lost their trade, when Europe captured big markets with the help of our cheap raw material converted into their final product by Industrial Revolution. They not only concealed their knowledge of 'Revolutionised Industry', but also blew off the simple 'Light of Life' (knowledge) in two ways-- a) by their least concern about improving Education, from Primary to Higher level and b) never thinking of leading us or training us towards Industrial Revolution. Literacy was shaded (forced down) to 5% even after their many promises for free and better Primary Education. It appears that the British Rulers were afraid of strengthening the people by Technical Education, just because it may lead again to Indian competition in machine articles and their trade. Six Universities, which they had opened, were non-teaching Universities with more prominence on English literature and not on technical subjects! They did not hesitate to close down ('not good') schools/colleges, instead of improving them. Even sanitation was not taken care of in many places; but they took care to lead the polluted or sewage water into the rivers-particularly to our holy river Ganga in the holy place of Kashi !! British Rulers always felt their budget money was insufficient for Education, Sanitation, Plague and Poor people; but they had enough budget for increasing the military strength and Railways. In short, their sudden ravages rattled the local Kings, rich persons and families also. Poverty and famines continued to hit the already poor people; their daily life was extremely disturbed, and the mind was always worried, dreaming about a bit better life, if not a good life. The Indian Rebellion (the first war of independence) of 1857 was a major uprising in India in 1857–58, against the East India Company. Queen's Proclamation (1858), also known as The Magna Carta, promised a lot, but the British Rulers in India didnot fulfill the requirements in full. The only option left was for the educated members of Indian National Congress (1885) to take up the problems as Resolutions placed before the Govt.

The worst of the treatments given to Indians by the British Officials can be seen in Pt. Malaviya's keen analysis as a Member of INC from 1886 onwards. British boasted about great improvements in India by introducing Railways and builidng Delhi as capital, and were happy for maintainig a big army at high expenditure to fight many wars (more wars outside our country) and the great World War in 1914. In spite of many requests by the educated persons (in Congress), the British group ignored even crucial problems for many decades from 1858 onwards also. Few Indian Kings were conquered and remained anxious and worried about the British military strength; but Indian Kings remained silent even when they lost quite a bit of their prosperity. One small example (out of many) is the frequent efforts (three/five times) by Britishers to win over Hyder Ali of Mysore State, with the support of other group of warriors. Each time the British claimed and recieved big fines of lakhs of rupees from Hyder Ali, before returning from the war. The cycle of imported Trade items to India (at high costs), wars to capture kingdoms, forcing for gratification funds from Indian rulers, (in place of their throne and land), sending Indentured Labour **of the worst form** to outside our country--- all these continued for a long time.

All these problems pained the members of Congress, but it seemed that no one else had any alternative to improve the worst situation, apart from frequent resolutions. It may not be an exaggeration to state that mainly Pt. Malaviya **analysed** most of all the difficult problems to the citizens of the country and also the possible solution. This is taken up in the next Chapter.

# Chapter -2

# ROLE OF Pt. MALAVIYA 

Pt. Madan Mohan Malaviya was aware of the problems during the British Rule from his early years and he also had the full opportunity to study the problems in detail from the time he became a Member of Indian National Congress in 1886. During the few centuries before 1886, our country was shattered in many ways as mentioned earlier. Service posts for Indians were shown as degraded clerks or Babus. Pt. Malaviya had come to the conclusion that the country's various problems could be overcome only by Education in Science and Technology and by experience in Industrial operations. As a strong spiritualist from his birth, Pt. Malaviya could also see that the back bone of the British country was combined in **War and Trade**, where as our country was strong in war and spirituality both, right from the time of Ramayan. (As already mentioned in page 8) this was symbolised in many shlokas (verses) like *"Sarve Bhavantu Sukhinah...."*-- They lived a life centered on Dharma, backed up by calmness of **Peace and Piety.** These spiritual persons, mostly Sanyasis, would also guide the disturbed poor people, who suffered the pains and problems of the turmoil, faced from outside. Inspite of the fear of the invaders or enemies, these Sanyasis and common people spent their life as calmly as possible with 'Peace and Piety', in the place of suffering in shaky turbulent world-- this was the strength of 'Spirituality'.

## Education-- Only Solace

Pt. Malaviya had noted the importance of Education

from Primary level to **Science and Technology,** in order **to** build Modern India **of Progress and Prosperity.** But he was clear that mere Education alone was not sufficient and it had to be joined with good Character of students. He was clear that 'Prosperity' would feed the five (hungry) sense organs to the (unreasonable) satisfaction of people; and if not cautious it will also go beyond the control of 'Ten Heads'. Where as 'Spirituality' (through **Sanatan Dharma)** would lead to **'Peace Piety'.** 'Spirituality'  would also take us more and more towards the Unity in any phase from home to the whole of Universe, as mentioned in 'Sanatan Dharma' by Annie Besant & Bhagavan Das-p-167.

When we follow the **'Best of the West'**, the material resources would increase to meet the never-ending cravings of human beings, meet the external satisfaction (of our five physical elements- five sense organs- like eye, ear etc).This is natural not only in the West, but of all the people every where, with practically no restrictions. The main difference in our country is the support of Dharma that would indicate the set of strong Rules (depending on the five *Indriyas*) to improve **Character** of the students, who would otherwise become keen mainly on **Best of the West** education only. These Rules that forbid us to cross certain lines during and after eduaction is known as Dharma. Since  'Dharma' is in vogue from times immenorial, it is called as Sanatan Dharma, and Pt. Malaviya has called it as the **Best of the East**. Again to repeat, Sanatana Dharma gives the rules for good living for the self, the family, the society, the country etc, as mentioned earlier. This is shown as 'Strengthening Minds', deeds (do's and dont's) within the ethics (not the view points of different religions) laid out by age old Sanatan Dharma.

# Chapter - 3

# STRENGTHENING SPIRITUALITY*

## *SANATAN DHARMA

## *Spirituality-Piety-Piousness--to equanimate or soften the rough waves of 'Prosperity'

Rough waves of the sea can not be slowed down by man where as, rough waves of 'Prosperity' of a person are like the waves of the mind. These waves of mind can be controlled by Spirituality, which controls the five sensors like Eye, Ear. Nose, Tongue and Touch. Sanatan Dharma followed in all ways is like the control of the mind and the rough waves.

Pt. Malaviya had seen most of the problems in the Country during the British Rule; also how to get out of poverty by improving 'Education' (from Primary to University level) and Development of Industries so that people are employed to a good extent. The Government was not caring much to improve **Education** at different levels, (with six non-teaching Universities), even after a number of requests over years from 1885 to 1904/1916. Pt. Malaviya **might have** felt the need of a separate University from many years earlier like-- a) when he was a teacher in school (1884-1886), b) when he heard and discussed many times on 'Education' during IN.Congress sessions 1886-1902; c) when permission was requested in 1902 to start Tata Institute. Later he decided in 1904 to open a University to improve the situation. For various reasons, his effort to establish Benares Hindu University was delayed upto 1916. The main 'Objectives' of the University, as clearly specified by Pt. Malaviya were two--that the University should concentrate on --

1. **Best of the West** for Science & Technology, resulting in **Progress & Prosperity** of the the Country

2. **Best of the East** to ensure that students understand the spirituality through Sanatan Dharma and get used to **good Character**, thereby smoothly balancing between **Prosperity and Piety** during the future working days.

(**Note**--After the above brief discription of Pt. Malaviya's explanations, an attempt is made to give the expected results of the two **Objectives of the University.**

## Best of The West

### Progress and Prosperity Lead - To Attraction and Addiction

Best of The West-Progress and Prosperity Lead - To Attraction and Addiction. The more one stresses on worldly Progress and Prosperity, the more will be the hunger for ever-changing, never decreasing enjoyments in worldly matters. And the enjoyment is for satisfying the five Indriyas (sensory organs) of persons, all of which happen to be pointing/looking only outwards. The more one sticks or enjoys the outside matter only, the more is the attraction towards it (or its other varieties). The simple attraction turns into wide addiction (like a 'wild weed' which is very tough to break), difficult to cut or tear it. Instead of cutting the weed of attraction, the person will be more involved in madly circling around, again and again, to some how catch his itching desires. When the enjoyment is missed or turned back (from any of the five indriayas), the sorrow covers him like a dark cloud. It is natural that the sensory organs enjoy what avails outside only. For his happiness, man depends on his relatives, friends and for his lust he does not hesitate to jump into a deep well to catch the good look or attraction. Imagine Ravana with ten heads, ie having lust ten or hundred times more than any other Asuras!!

Those depending only on the happiness from outside life, have to soon suffer from sorrow; but yet they keep searching more outside only.

**Few Examples** -- are of Ravana, Duryodhana and many others--who were never satisfied with accumulation of treasure, pleasure, power, hatred, ego, taste and lust-- all for temporary satisfaction and enjoyment! They had enough of every thing to quench their (ever dry, ever open, ever smelling, ever bragging, ever lustful) five sensories in all possible ways; yet they would hungrily jump (like a tiger) on any newly found matter of their choice. This was the endless extreme of the players who stuck to sensories; the other extreme was that of the Kumbhakarna, who used to close his eyes for six months at a time and opened lately for drinks - drugs and food of unmeasurable quantity at a time!

**Today's World** - has multiplied the different attractions (towards five sensories) in unmanageable fast and vast ways, in contrast to what were available hundred years back. A small example is of foods, drinks, drugs, entertainments etc which are of thousands of varieties more than the earlier; they are there now to attract the rich or poor, young or old, healthy or unhealthy, honest or dishonest, devotee/sadhu or thief or goonda. Similarly, the minor attraction (of the earlier times) appreciating a 'shy female' dancer in a village drama can no more be compared to the present day 'world beauties ' dancing in cinema or TV or  in a closed door show. Five sensories (of today's people) attract most of the human beings in different ways, just like the honeybee are attracted in groups.  One has to be carefully far away from the sharp bee-sting or a snake bite. Spirituality is the only way of looking inside and not playing and looking outside to satisfy the Sensors, as mentioned now!!

## ESSENTIAL TO CHANGE

Sri Krishna has said in Gita-"In this world of daily unhappiness, you pray to me (9.33)". There is also an explanation saying --that Sri Krishna is in the inside (*Antharanga*) of all, as the Divyatma (Divine Spirit) of supreme happiness. In short, the message is that the man has to turn the vision from outside to inside (*Antharanga*) to get supreme happiness!

Rishis mention about Sanatan Dharma and say that the man should hold the way to *Antharanga* or the inner side; this only saves one from the outer circle of happiness and the next cyclone of sorrow. This change does not mean that one has to forsake the family or society; it means a change in the orientation of lifestyle --the synthesis or coordination of *Antharanga* and *Bahiranga*--it is the foundation of Sanatan Dharma, "a set of principles of a healthy and beneficent life". To win or pass over the difficulties and sorrows, one has to look inside and try to know the Paramatma.(Ref-Purusha Sukta) Just like the turtle, which can quickly withdraw all its organs, the *Stitaprajna* (firm minded) withdraws all his organs (sensory) from the worldly matters. This is the only way to be away from sorrow and melancholy, as per Sanatan Dharma (Annie Besant & Bhagavan Das p-1).

In between Ravana and Kumbhakarna was Vibhishana, who could easily turn his looks away from the six qualities (*Shadgunas*) (Roopa; Rasa, Gandha, Shabda, Sparsha and Maithuna) and look within towards **Antaraatma** (the internal spirit or Paramatma, who is in the heart of all) in search of **Amrutatva** (or immortality). This look inside is not just the vision of the eyes, (but it is closing the gates of the five sensory organs) and turn all that power (of all sensory organs) towards inside. It means turning the power of sensory organs into awesome power of resignedness (or **Vairagya**). This change is not easy at all.

It requires the mind and the **Jnana** to be absolutely clean and pure. (This change from sensory-stuck mind to spiritual mind ---is explained in **Kathopanishat**)

<u>**Tough British Rule & Education Ignored & Pushed 'Prosperity' To Ditch--**</u> --Unfortunately, our country was thrown down badly from its earlier climax of 'Prosperity' into the dirty ditch of poverty, bad health, low literacy (5%), no work or earnings, no avenues to rescue from plagues and famines, no education and no step or sympathy from Government (in spite of their many promises for free education etc - As mentioned earlier). Hiding the European Industrial Revolution (1760-1840), from reaching India was the main reason for the calamity of Indian trade and other connected problems shown so far. Whatever be the type of problems, Pt Malaviyaji considered **Education** as the starting step for gradual rescue and improvements. Therefore, he stressed on <u>**Education**</u> (at that time) from Primary upto very essential Science & Technology for general 'Progress and Prosperity' through development of different industries, agriculture, trade, providing jobs to people, who had no other option.

(Note--small repititions to confirm earlier thoughts)

Pt. Malaviya had much to explain about Education. He quoted ancient Manu, that "Wealth, Relations, Age, Good Deeds and Learnings" are the five titles that get respect more in the reverse way -- so that 'Learning' will be of utmost respect and 'Wealth' in the fifth place. (INC1909-Lahore). Since illiteracy and ignorance were the root of all problems, he wanted the education to reach the masses and develop the youth with ancient ideals of spirituality, moral ethics and Indian ideals -- then only the Youth would develop National spirit. While he wished to use the best elements of English education, he did not like the imitation of the culture/customs of the West. He wanted a new curriculum (along with the main subjects of study) to instill in the students the idea of self help and to build up the character in youth. He was keen on balanced training of body, intellect and the feeling and emotions of student. This included a) to build up health and strength of body and mind, b) emotional training, and c) scientific, technical and professional knowledge, and practical training for indigenous industries, d) character of youth through religion, ethics based on **Sanatan Dharma**-- initiation into a life of spirit, training of souls in the pursuit of truth and practice of virtue. He preferred inculcation of self-discipline in students. Pt. Malaviya did not want our people to be stuck to 'Prosperity' only. He wanted them to be spiritual also. Whatever be the new way of living (may be as King, Trader, Teacher, or even uneducated person), he should not forget Dharma or the right way of living, that was spread out in the atmosphere of his own life.

**Pujya Mahuli Gopalacharya** (of Satyadhyana Vidyapeetha, Mumbai) in his book "The Insights" on Sanatan Dharma has given a clear frank picture of the many changes that take place to our culture, as long as the <u>western copy of civilization goes hand in hand with our culture.</u> Following paragraph gives his views--these are similar to Pt. Malaviya's views.

<u>Effect of Copying</u> Western **Education---Our** social customs are abhorred, elders are defied; universal revolt against God, religion and eternal values. More of these happen as students get into higher class-- First there is indifference to Values, next occasional falsehood, and then studied mendacity (untruthfulness) --progress on the road of foul play and dishonesty. (For more details of this writing, pl see page 33--Appendix <u>5. Sanatan Dharma, "The Insights" by Pujya Mahuli Gopalacharya)</u>

<u>**Brief About Sanatan Dharma**</u> 'Sanatan' means eternal Supreme Soul (which is begining-less and endless) and always existent, not a human being. Sanatan **Dharma** is that which saves us, from all sorts of destructions or degradation and leads up, means that which is coming from immemorial or that which is of permanent nature or eternal and inherent. It does not possess a limited and narrow meaning like the word 'Religion'. <u>Dharma is that which holds the entire system of creation. The entire creation is held together and sustained by the Law. The practice of Dharma means to recognise the laws and abide by them</u>. He who violates the principles of Dharma meets destruction and who acts in consonance with it leads a happy life. Man's duty lies in doing good to all creatures, irrespective of any classification -- it means maintaining order in the world, making all other creatures happy.

Adharma leads to destruction and does harm now or later. As Tulsi Das says--"O brother, there is no virtue equal to doing good to others, and nothing **so as to inflict pain on others**" And the Gita says-"The Yogi restraining and subduing the sences, looks upon everything with an equal eye, and devotes himself to the good of all creatures, --he attains Me"

Ten qualities attributed to Dharma (by Manu) are-Patience, Forgiveness, Restraint, Non-stealing, Purity, Control Over Sense-Organs, Talent, Knowledge, Truthful, and Absence of Anger.

# Chapter - 4

# MORE EXPLANATION OF 'SANATAN DHARMA'

## SRI SRI BHARATHI TEERTHA MAHASWAMI JI, JAGADGURU, DAKSHINAMNAYA SRI SHARADA PEETHAM, SRINGERI.

*(More explanations help in better understanding)

**Definitions To Understand 'Dharma'**

(Most of the portions are taken from the Kannada Book **'Sanatan Dharma-Part 1, which itself is entirely based on Jagadguru's Speeches over a number of days)**

**<u>Avoid Arguements & Accept Almighty</u>**

**(Also Speaks of Discipline To Be Maintained by Students)**

**God-** There is no point to question whether God is there or not!! He is all powerful, the whole creation (*Brahmaanda*) and its nurture is by Him. Not a small piece of grass grows without His clearance. He is the One to either grace you with happiness or give you sorrow. He is the base of the principles-(Tattva) and the right way of living- Dharma. The whole *Brahmaanda* ultimately joins Him during the final flood (or *Pralaya*). It is not possible to explain Him in few words.

**Upanishads-** One can read the theories of **Upanishads** in order to clearly-firmly understand the teachings of Vedas.

**Smritis** are an essence of Vedas. They preach in a brief way of what is preached in the Vedas. Smritis were written by Rishis - Manu, Yajnavalkya and Parashara--they have given a shape to Vedas.

shape to Vedas. *Aachara Samhite* are well organised codes, based on the above Smritis of three Rishis. Thus, Veda, Smriti and Shastraachara are the firm base of Dharma.

**Exposition of Vedas and Dharma--** Dharma by Vedas should not be objected through arguements, a) Students should never belittle or comment or make a laughing stock after the Guru completes his teaching, b) Even by mistake, one should not get into unwanted arguements on Vedas, c) Should not use one's (assumed) bright thinking and intelligence to argue, review and find fault with teaching, d) Bad logic, unwanted logic in *Shruti* etc should not be carried on, e) Feeling that he himself is a great scholar and saying that his bright logic can not be defeated etc are incorrect-- this will badly exhibit his proud nature, f) He will not realise that there could be another Pandit to beat him in such unwanted arguements!

**Vedas -- Sanatana Dharma** is embedded firmly in the Vedas. They are ideal and holy scriptures with supreme power on Dharma, which is not spelled by the man; not the written volumes; not of any specific writer; it has neither a beginning nor an end; it is known as the breath (*Praanavaayu*) of Shiva. Study and practice of Vedas can only enable us to understand the essence of Dharma. One is supposed to study the branch of Vedas, as per tradition, and that has to be followed. (Earlier there were 24 *Shaakhas* or branches in Rigveda, 101 in Yajurveda, 1000 in Samaveda and 9 in Atharvaveda. Now, all *Shaakhas* / branches together have 8-10 branches). Supreme Lord (God) has graced us the Vedas for the good of the world and the welfare of all the human beings.
Paramatma to Hiranyagarbha (Vedas) to Rishis (branches or Smritis) to us as per Heritage.

**Vedas are** the powers showing the way of Dharma. Vedas have the unquestionable, unequal power to decide on the format of Dharma. It is like the sun-light identifying any

matter (not needing some other light). No body else can think of getting this power to format Dharma (with his own interpretation and explanation). Sri Shankaracharya said--
"if any such situation comes in the way, the world will go towards full of confusion and destruction".

**God Brings Back Sanatan Dharma** -- through incarnations of Sri Rama in Treta Yug; Sri Krishna in Dwapar Yug; Sri Shankara in Kali Yug. In the first two incarnations, the evil persons were killed. Sri Shankara opened the eyes of those who were anti-Dharma, opposers of Dharma, those against Shastras--by opening their eyes by avakening Dharma in people. There is another saying--**"If the world has to be prosperous, Dharma has to be implemented. Then Dharma alone gives welfare and people will be happy"**

**Sri Shankara**-- Sri Shankara gave a powerful preaching in a sentence--*"Lokah Smastaha Sukhino Bhavantu"* meaning --**May Good Happen to All; May There Be Welfare to All, May All be always in Noble Ways.** He established four eminent places for the Guru to occupy the seat (the *Peetha*) in the four directions of the country. The main objectives were a) in order to spread Dharma all over and continuously, b) the tradition of Gurus to be continued. and c) that every one should be involved in Sanmarga (noble ways of living). The spread of Dharma is very excellent, very rare elsewhere. After 1200 years also the Shankara institution is running well to meet his objectives.

**Sanatan Dharma-- Basic Principles to be followed**--Full belief in God and his re-incarnation; complete deligence (*Shraddha*) in Vedas; behaving with love in the family and to live happily in the society. (The best way to convert the Mind from outside to *Antharanga* or inside)

**Sanatan Dharma**--is dharma that has been eternal or

perennial, with no definite time or period of its beginning. This has neither the beginning nor the end of it, which is infinity and like a permanent burning fire. It combines all and take them in the only Dharma to continue the heritage, to bestow the good to all.

**Dharma -- A set of principles** for a healthy and beneficient life (of living beings or the existence of world). **Observance of Dharma-**results in peace and piety for the person, for the good of him in his life, resulting in continuous happiness; it takes one away from the cycles of 'happiness and sorrow' from the five sensory organs. Any fault in the observance of Dharma leads to the opposites like poverty, grief and unhappy/disturbed life. The entire world prevails on following Dharma and failure to follow it results in chaos and calamity. Dharma is pleasant for the individual, the family, the society and the whole world. If the world has to be prosperous, Dharma has to be implemented; then Dharma alone gives welfare and people will be happy.

If the principles of Dharma are followed and people follow Dharma in practice, then there will be peace and happiness. Vedas have imposed only Dharma and nothing else; no other person or books will have this promise. This is the basic Tattva (principle) of Sanatan Dharma. If this power to decide on Dharma is handed over to the man, then there will be only confusion and difference of opinions between persons (leading to neglect of Dharma and heavy disputes)**Dharma-- Best Foundation--** Human being is the supreme amongst all the 84 Lakh living beings. For him Dharma is the **best foundation for his life** in the world. It **gives him permanent happiness and peace.** Without following Dharma no happiness can be experienced. When Dharma is left out or disregarded, then his fall starts off. One, who disregards Dharma or considers that it has no place in happy life, is really a fool above all other fools. He cannot escape from sorrow, he has to bear it. Similarly the **one, who discards Dharma before his Scientific intelligence, is a greater fool of high order.**

**Importance of Dharma**- Dharma is essential for man. His intense desire is to have a happy life now and in the next birth also, with no sorrow in any birth. If happiness is wanted and not sorrow, follow Dharma; because Dharma or Adharma is the reason for Happiness or Sorrow. This has been clearly said in the Vedas and Shaastras. Observance of Dharma is essential for every one--whether he is worker, scholar, rich person or the king. Ours is a prime land of Dharma. All previous generations have lived their life mainly on the basis of Dharma. They firmly believed that nothing can be achieved from the wealth coming from Adharma. Justice, honesty, sincerity, truth and Dharma are the breath of Bharathiyas.

**Follow Dharma Shaastra --**Just like law and rules are there to live in the world, the Shaastras also have certain rules for the goodwill. There is no need to know the person/group who wrote the law, but we have to follow according to the rule. In the same way, there is no need to know who wrote the Dharma Shaastra; it is our duty to live as per the Dharma Shaastra. An example is of a thief defending his action--"There was need for food at home and I had to get some money. Normally I do not steel, but if I aim forced to do, I will steel from wealthy person who has plenty of black money"

It is also not right to say that the subtle Dharma Shaastra has to be same for one and all. For example--the Shaastra says--Unmarried Brahmachari to follow subtle Indriya Nigraha; for the monk-Sanyasi, even a thought in the mind about lust is a big crime (*Paapa*). Similarly, non-violence is a big Dharma in the case of animals; but not so in the case of treatment of a patient.

When **worldly affairs are stuck strongly to the body-mind-five sensors**, it is difficult to bow down to ascetism (*Vairagya*). **There is always fear at every worldly step** like----fear of disease in lust, fear of  loosing job when employed,  fear of thieves when having money, fear of dishonour when holding privileged honour, afraid of enemy when strong also, beautiful one worried about old age, good person fearing shame, knowledgeable one fearing counterfeit-opponent,  body worried about death.... (Barthrahari)---**<u>All fears reduce when not too much is attached to worldly affairs and follow good habits of Dharma.</u>**

(**NOTE**--Many books have come out on the subject of "Sanatan Dharma". Most of them convey the same explanations with minor differences.)

<u>Summarised Explanations Of Dharma-</u>

(Details taken from Sri  Sri Bharathi Teertha  Maha Swamiji, from his speeches)

Veda, Smriti and Shaastra-Aachara are the  firm base of Dharma.

Vedas have imposed only Dharma and nothing else; no other person or books will   have this promise.

**If the world has to be prosperous, Dharma has to be implemented**

**Dharma alone gives welfare and people will be happy Sri Shankara -- "*Lokah Smastaha Sukhino Bhavantu*"**

meaning May good happen to all;  May there be welfare to all; May all be always in noble ways.

**A set of principles** of Dharma for healthy and beneficient life, if followed in practice, then there will be peace and happiness.

**Observance of Dharma** - results in peace and piety for the person, for the good of him in his life, resulting in continuous happiness; it takes one away from the cycles of 'Happiness and Sorrow' from the five sensory organs.

Dharma alone gives welfare and people will be happy.

Dharma is pleasant for the individual, the family, the society and the whole world

If happiness is wanted and not sorrow, follow Dharma; because Dharma or Adharma is the reason for Happiness or Sorrow. Observance of Dharma is essential for every one--whether he is worker, scholar, rich person or the king

Nothing can be achieved from the wealth coming from *Adharma*. Justice, honesty, sincerity, truth and Dharma are the breath.

When worldly affairs are stuck strongly to the body-mind-five sensors, it is difficult to bow down to ascetism (*Vairagya*).

(Details given by others are shown in the Appendix)

# Chapter - 5

# BROAD OUTLOOK OF 'SANATAN DHARMA'

## SRI SRI BHARATHI TEERTHA MAHASWAMI JI
JAGADGURU, DAKSHINAMNAYA SRI SHARADA PEETHAM, SRINGERI (Speeches Condensed),

**Broad Outlook** includes the different facets of Sanatan Dharma and also the broad way of following Sanatan Dharma.

**Practice To Work With Dharma**

1._ Prayer to God, repeating the name of the Lord, all these are for the man alone, not for the other living beings. One who does not follow this good opportunity as a human being is really a big fool. His human life is wasted.

2. Human life is like a boat trying to pass the ocean over a long time. The cycle of birth and death is the Ocean of Sorrow. Human body itself is the boat taken to cross the Ocean of Sorrow. If we do not fulfill our aim, we may again be born as animals. The aim of the human life can be fruitful only by **Jnana or knowlege**, and not from anything else.

**Control of Mind**

1. Mind has to be always in our control. Anger is a big enemy for the man; he bursts out to do wrong actions and later on will repent for his talk or action. But to say that one has to control himself and be silent/patient during a war with the enemy, it is wrong.

2. Helping others is good-sacred; but to torture him later on is forbidden.

3. Uttering Truth is good some times and silence only is good some other times. We have always to do any work to the inner feelings-witness of the mind.

4. Give acceptance to the Self-Witness and keep away the bad thoughts. <u>**Nourish Dharma**</u>--If we have to become followers of Dharma in life, it is essential to have certain obligations (binding promise, compulsions) in the life. Some are mentioned here-

1. **Protect Dharma and Dharma Protects You** -- Observe Dharma with belief that it is of great value-and there is nothing beyond it; so that the loyalty and confidence grows stronger to observe it without fail.

2. **Do Your Own Duty--** Few examples are -- parents serving the child, teacher guiding the student, the couple serving each other and the family, not to harm/trouble any one by talk or work, not to disturb or give pain to minds of others, not to steal other's material, not to tell lies or false dramas.

**More Sayings about Dharma**--Physical happiness and pleasure are illusions, they are let-down or upset only; keep away false thoughts/imaginations, live a life of Dharma for peace and happiness.

Dharma followed strictly will uplift the world into great hights (said Bhoj Raja)

In the begining of creation, God created the human being; He taught him the spiritual way of living. If this way followed carefully, the God would be happy- there would be rains in proper times, good crops etc would be given by God (Sri Krishna).

**Avoid Ego-Pride** leading to arrogance should not be there -- as this leads one to downfall (like Duryodhana). Don't be proud about money (richness), youngage, beauty, physical strength etc.

Krishna said to Arjuna on pride-"it is your illusion". There is no meaning to Ego-Pride; even a donor or benefactor should be silent and away from boasting or blowing one's own trumpet. Nothing is constant in life-- depend only on the Lord-Bhagavanta.

**Donate** with Good Feelings- A believer in God, known as Astika, should follow Dharma, help others, donate with good feelings (in mind) to those who are eligible--these lead to noble/great rebirth and then to heaven. Richness or any good thing is 'God given' and it has to be **quietly spent** in the name of His Service with the feeling-"Every thing is yours....." . A dis-believer in God or Nastika does not believe in any thing and feel everything is for his own enjoyment.

Sun was not happy when sea water was withdrawn; Sun made the vapour of water and gave enough water in the form of rain to man. Rains came because we did Homa and followed Dharma (Kalidasa)

The foundation stone for the entire world was the decent Dharma. We become befitting for the world, only when we follow Dharma. We cannot be fit here with thousand talks and thousnad works.

It is not possible, if we think that the keeping of our hands in fire would not burn. The hands will burn.

Dharma only will be of help when one is internaly disturbed, troubled by fear and confusions. For such persons Dharma is the guide for the right path, giving patience and peace of mind and saviour of life. The observance of Dharma is listed in Vedas-Shaastras; therefore they have to be followed with diligence.

**Continue Heritage** (many points to be noted) a) it has to be continued/carried on with its same old dignity and the road shown by seniors on the basis of their righteousness and and Shastras,

b) not to ignore or break it with bad beliefs, dirty or unwanted arguements, mistaken imaginations, c) not becoming an enemy or a person with hatred to the society, d) not getting into useless meaningless talks and cursing or making fun of own ancestors.

**Maintain Culture** by service to society and to the God in the name of God. a) The first lesson of Culture is full belief in God, confidence and bhakti in Him, no short coming or half-hearted view, b) no arrogance and pride, c) avoid arguements with unwanted logic,  without enemity, without ego and selfishness, service to society, d) maintain heritage to bestow good to all e) take away the cycle of 'happiness and sorrow' from the five sensory organs to get permanent happiness and peace.

Be close with His Grace -- Good ways are- a) to keep your mind free by praying for his grace, b) open your mind freely in the assembly of devotees, c) spend time where the ascetic (*Tapasvi*) is in prayer or pooja, d)  help in some work connected with the maintenance of temple, e) maintain love in family, happy in sociey, keep principles for healthy and beneficient life.  God is the father of all, we are all His children; there is no senior or no better or no greater than Him,  He is the one to be worshipped; He is the One to grace us, protect us.

**Not Against Culture**- One who does not agree to above principles is not considered as a human being. One who discards Dharma before scientific intelligence is a great fool of high order. **It is not Culture** a) to pretend and show off for fashion, b) expose his ego as a respectable senior and proud person with high thoughts/behaviour--c)always claiming that his points are correct and the others are not, d) abusive talks, thoughts and negligence towards God to show off in parade or to scream and show off in assembly for gaining popurality,  e) atheistic arguements (like--"if God is helpless or silent when

the mouse runs over the Linga, how can we believe God?")
and why pray him with flowers and pooja!etc! Similarly, f) it
is indecent--not decorous to-  object the Vedas in any way,
either objection or making fun of the teaching after the Guru
taught the Veda, or using one's own intelligence for unwanted
arguement or scandal or fallacy.

**Always Remember Culture -** Culture is important. We
are human beings. We have some rules-written or passed on by
Heritage. We have a Dharma to follow,  a system to continue.
We have to follow them properly. Keep this feeling with you,
follow the Heritage with love (not by force or compulsion).
That  feeling and love to follow heritage is Dharma-Veda.There
is nothing older than Veda. If Shveta Kalpa is running now,
there was definitely another Kalpa before the present one.
Vedas were also there earlier. That is why, there are no
mistakes of Kalpas in Vedas. The Vedas teach us the system of
Dharma  for our life; take the man to the high status and then
inform even the way to get the state of Moksha. If you have the
aspiration for Moksha, keep away from routine subject matter.
**<u>Be Careful</u> -Decay of Dharma--**

**1)** One who does not learn and understand knowledge
(jnana) and prosperity of Dharma. 2) One who does not follow
the principles of Dharma, will have to face difficulties.
Examples-- Of the Satvik or Rajasik or Tamasik Food, Satvik is
good for Dharma.

3) Opposing Vedas has become a practice of the day--.
a) It is like saying that the food served by mother is not good
and prefering to go to hotel;
b) Feeling now a days that going in the correct way does not
give a penny of money;
c) Going in a way different from Shaastras with a feeling that
would get huge amounts;
d) Eating food normally forbidden;  e) married couple, instead

of happy united ways, go according to their own individual wishes and in bad lanes;

f) split in society under differential groups by language, caste rituals, etc

g) forgetting that we have to have confidence in God, a confidence flowing in the same way as the Ganga flow, and finding it difficult to forget the splits;

h) a dry arguement to say that our civilisation has grown well and positively;

i) the so-called principles of modern civilisation may again be crashed away by still more intelligent and more knowledgeble persons in future.

**Decay of Dharma**, as mentined above, has given a strong feeling that the Hindu Culture has long ceased to be like a living river. Culture mixed with present Progress and Prosperity appears to be getting into a fen (marsh land) of stagnant waters. Boasting as of the longest life and history, it has had its proper growth arrested, its further development nearby is choked. Do not be fancied about different Culture, just because of your work/stay away from our Country or when one becomes friendly with an outsider due to work or reason.

**Bad Demonstrations of Dharma**--Do a bad job laughingly; experience that fruit cryingly. If one shows off or continues in a different way, but acts like a good person, good manners, but think and work in a bad way---in that case he is fooling himself. Three temptations for sin are **Woman, Wealth and Wine** (and all W's combined in a stay in foreign country or when one becomes friendly with a group in work or social activities). One who knows his mistakes/wrong doings and yet does it --is a blind one. One who has heard a preaching and yet ignores it to do a wrong thing is a dumb fellow. Listen to some one's pride, copy his bad practices-even not to his dignity, then this copying is like a screen to good thoughts.

# Chapter - 6

# HOW TO FOLLOW 'SANATAN DHARMA'

## SRI SRI BHARATHI TEERTHA MAHASWAMI JI, JAGADGURU, DAKSHINAMNAYA SRI SHARADA PEETHAM, SRINGERI.

**Five Simple Formulas**

1) Not to trouble others, 2) Not to say false, 3) Not to steal anything, 4) Consider all ladies, excepting the wife, as your mothers, 5) Not to be greedy for every thing seen.

**Five Tips To Remember**

1) Lust and Life for worldly matters do not give any sacred Punya.

2) Wealth, Authority, Knowledge are all negligable in life. It is not Paramartha.

3) Wealth, Authority, Knowledge cannot be taken as the only aim of life.

4) Effort for Spiritual Achievement for next birth should be the aim.

5) Practice of Dharma to be initiated early for a good /holy birth next time.

**Three Firm Beliefs**

1) Maintain Reverence to Shastra and the teaching of Guru.

2) Have full faith in *Jaganmaate* during problems.

3) Do Not come down from Unswerving Faith, Unshakeble Bhakti, Reverance Prayer.

**Three Sins**

1. When one aspires/wishes for happiness, instead of puttting effort to do good work--- changing the purpose/aim to any work of sins in order avoid sorrow-- is a big sin.

2.   To decide what is good work and what is not by oneself, leads to anarchy. One's thoughts may be different from others. Therefore to think over and come to a good/correct solution, there has to be a **basis of Shaastras** (rather than blind decision by self or with others).

3. There are ten types of sins--think in the mind about other's wealth and posession; think and talk about doing harm to others; think of bad lust to satisfy the body in unwanted ways etc.  <u>**Four Accessories**</u> **(Saadhana Chatustaya)**--

1. Prudence-Judiciousness, (Viveka); 2) Asceticism (Vairagya); 3) Shama-Damadi Saadhana; 4) Mumukshatva

(Pl  NOTE- So Far "**Sanatan Dharma**" Part-1 has been taken from many speeches by **Sri Sri Bharati Teertha Maha Swamiji**, Jagadguru-Dakshinamnaya Sri Sharada Peetha, Sringeri. More of 'Formulas' are given here, again from same source, but from the point of Spirituality).

# BE SPIRITUAL

<u>**Five Senses**</u>

1.  Do not get caught up always with 5 Senses--Eye, Ear, Nose, Tongue and Touch. All five are attached to wordly life (*Bahiranga*). No worldly matter can give permanent satisfaction or happiness. ( Just like a sweet in the tongue, eyes at a beauty, ears for a song---)

2.  More the senses indulge to stick to their choice, the quicker is the break down from pleasure to reach sorrow (like from health to disease).

3.  Hunger for ever-changing enjoyments,  is like hunting a bird  or  wolf  for  needs  or  a  deer  or  tiger  for recreation//amusement--such multiplied attractions lead to more casualities (unknown dangers). Number of choices for happiness//enjoyments (in the present world) are like selecting a saree in a big 'Saree Street' for the beloved!

4. All the sensories feed the mind, fill it up, mix it badly, confuse actions and darken the road (each in its own way) and mislead the way, so that the planned goal does not reach.

5. One who wants to pick honey from the tree, gets many bites by a group of bees.

**6.** Mind can take a person to the aspiration of a Happy World, a Heavenly World! Such a person should jump into the deep pond of Mind, deep into his own imagination and reach the bottom where the poisonous snake (of lust and passion) lies down and <u>ensnare it by the Jap of  Mantras, knock it down</u> quickly and thereby clean the Mind! This was the way Krishna hit the poisonous snake in the river!!

7. The five sense organs touching the Mind may be anything of dirty sight, bad sound etc. They dislodge the Mind and divert it towards anything of "Kama, Krodha, Moha, Madha, Lobha, Matsarya, Dvesha, Lajje, Bhaya, Sukha, Dukkha, Utsaaha, Nirutsaaha, Sankalpa". All this is due to the worldly matters. The only way to see that these bad ugliness does not stick firmly, the only way is to lower down the play with worldly attachments, and get more involved in **spirituality.---Thus, as Sri Krishna says--this** *Bahiranga* **is a world of unhappiness**

## Be Inclined Towards Spirituality-

**1.** Whether you look in towards Divya Atma for a short time or more, whether you pray or be silent, you will be away from the (above) worldly five of problems and unhappiness.

2 Look inside of yourself, towards the *Antaranga*- the place of Divya Atma- the Lord of your love-the Supreme Happiness.

3 Learn to withdraw all external looking sensories, withdrawing like a turtle withdrawing in a second before a sign of hurt is traced; be away from the worldly touch, from the glimpse of attraction or melancholy.

4. More you turn in and practice to look inside, (whether all alone, or while in front of a Lord in your Lord's Room, or in a temple) the more you look and pray, the less will be the trace of Worldly Unhappiness.

**5. Antaranga is a world of Calmness-Happiness--and the entry into it, requires the permission of Lord!! Spend a Few Minutes For Prayer To Your Lord!**

6. A mind disturbed by a worry on external matters will spoil the sleep for long time. Filling up the mind with a deep thought (a silent continuous prayer) will give solace, followed by sleep.

**(NOTE) Waking up** after a sound sleep, the morning may suddenly be followed by a disorderly world (seen in the news items or phones or by any other problems hitting you). This sudden disorder touching your mind is similar to a **"Fly Giving Fungus From Garbage"** in a second!! or a **"Bee Giving Honey From Tree and a big prick before you get a drop of honey"** !!

**7.  Stick to Three Firm Beliefs-**

a) Unswerving Faith, Unshake-able Bhakti, and Reverance Prayers.

b) Have full faith in **Jagannatha/ Jaganmaate** in all times and during problems.

c) Reverence to **Shaastra and The Teachings of Guru.**

# Chapter - 7

# 'SANATAN DHARMA'
# Pt. MALAVIYA'S POLICY FOR BHU

We now come to the two important goals of Banaras Hindu University --

1. **Best of West** in Science & Techology as the basis for **Progress and Prosperity** of the country and the welfare of the poverty/famine stricken people as a whole, so that they **build Modern India** from the shattered country

2. **Best of East** with Sanatan Dharma as the basis of **Peace and Piety** to support the inner personality of the students, by following Dharma, Traditions, Culture, Customs, Heritage etc so that the students keep up the high character, probity and honour **to strengthen the spirituality in the country.**

Few sayings of Pt. Malaviya explain further on the above two objectives-

"It is my earnest hope and prayer that this centre of life and light, which is coming into existence, will produce students who will <u>not only be intellectually</u> equal to the best of their fellow students in other parts of the world, but will also live a <u>noble life, love their country</u> and be loyal to the Supreme ruler."

"BHU will seek not merely to turn out men as engineers, scientists, doctors, merchants, theologians, but also as men of high character, probity and honour, whose conduct through life will show that they bear the hall-mark of a great University"

"We are watching to-day the birth of a new and, many hope, a better type of University in India. The main features of this University, which distinguish it from existing Universities, will be, first, that it will be a teaching and residential University; secondly, that while it will be open to all castes and creeds, it will insist upon religious instruction for Hindus, and thirdly, that it will be conducted and managed by the Hindu community and almost entirely by non officials"

" A teaching university would but half perform its function <u>if it does not seek to develop the **heart power**</u> of its scholar with the same solicitude with which it would <u>develop their **brain power**</u>."

"I believe, instructions in the **truths of religion**, whether it would be Hindus or Mussalmans, whether it be imparted to the students of Banaras Hindu University or of the Aligarh Moslem University, will tend to produce men who, if they are <u>true to their religion</u>, will be true to their God, their King and their country. And I look forward to the time when the students who will pass out of such Universities, will meet each other in a closer embrace as sons of the same Motherland than they do at present"

"University ought to be a place where the knowledge is always turned to good purposes, and where its boundaries are receiving a <u>constant extension</u>".. "where it turns out professionals who are men of high character, probity and honour."

**Dharma - The Righteous Path** –"People well versed in morals and firm in resolve do not get distracted from the righteous path whether they are abused or praised, wealth is gone or comes in, death comes calling today or waits for the turn of the century"

"Whatever you want for yourself, think that the same will be wanted by others also". (Shanti Parva, 59.22, Mahabharat,) and "To others we should not do something, which if done to you by others will hurt you"

(Vishnudharmottara Purana 3.255.44)---In brief, this is dharma, taught as **Reciprocity** by Malaviyaji. Beyond this, everything is done with the desire of something else.

<u>Values-</u> Malaviyaji said-"Development of human values alone is divinity. I am a believer in human values. I do not value caste and community above human values"

**Good Behaviour**—"Love for the good company of pious persons, liking for the good qualities in others, humility in front of teacher, interest in knowledge, love for one's wife, fear about bad name from society, devotion to Vishnu (or the God of your choice), strength of self control, freedom from the company of the wicked—in who so ever these pure qualities reside, my obeisance to that great soul"

"Work of those people will not be fruitful, who work with selfish feelings, malice and enmity. But where work is carried out with unselfish feelings there people seeing the success of some become happy; love and sympathy surface and the work will soon get its result. People with unselfish feelings term their work as God's work and God is their helper; they never get disheartened and sit back because of problems of obstacles".

"…..Love your countrymen and **promote unity** among them. A **large measure of toleration** and forbearance, and a larger spirit of **loving service** is demanded of you. …A remembrance of **your duty to your country** will help you always to be prepared to offer **any sacrifice which may be demanded of you for the protection of its interests or honour… "**

**Four Simple Principles -to improve physical energy --** In his frequent rounds in the campus, he always advised the students to follow **certain discipline** for 'character building'--Examples are given below-----

**Dudh peevo** ('Drink Milk'--stick to only **Satvik but nourishing food** or drinks),

**Kasrat Karo** ( 'Do Physical Exercise' so that the body is fit all the time and good spirits/feelings are maintained with others), **Pado** ('Read and Understand'-- to achieve the purpose for which you have come here -- (not to loiter and waste time), **Ram Naam Japo** ('Meditate' and practice *Bramhacharya* or celibacy- till 25 years- to improve '**Concentration**').

Pt. Malaviya wanted students to "worship God through <u>service to the poor countrymen</u> and love for all, clear the ignorance in the world, stop the deceit and exploitation and spread truth, tread the right path and show compassion to everyone and help generate mutual love, happiness and peace amongst people".......

"May you become eligible for the respect from the society through your truthfulness, brahmacharya, physical exercise, knowledge, patriotism and self sacrifice......Throughout the period of your work, take care to keep alive the **sense of your duty** towards God and towards your country. It will sustain you in the most difficult situations and help you to avoid the many obstacles which beset your path. A remembrance of what you owe to God will help you to <u>cherish feelings of brotherliness,</u> of kindness and compassion, not only towards men but towards all innocent creatures of God.....

" Life supported by good thoughts and decorated by good conduct only could be the best means for self-improvement and social welfare. <u>Inculcating patriotism</u> only can ensure the change for the good of nation. <u>Selfless patriotism</u> only can help carrying out real good service to the nation. Democratic principles and civilised behaviour only can make its people oriented, sustain and stabilise democracy."

There are many very popular sayings of Pt. Malaviyaji for

following Sanatan Dharma. Only few are given here-

दूध पियो, कसरत करो, नित्य जपो हरिनामा ।

हिम्मत से कारज करो, पूरेंगे सब काजा ।।

घट घट व्यापक राम जप रे, मत करो बैर, झूठ मत बाखै ।

मत पर धन हर, मत मद चाखै ।।

जीव मत मार, जुवा मत खेलै ।

मत पर तिय लख, यही तेरो तप रे ।।

Pt. Malaviya's advice to students goes beautifully thus (repeated)--

Ghat Ghat Vyaapak Ram Jap Re, Mat Kar Bair,

Jhoot Mat Baakhai,

Mat Par Dhan Har, Mat Mad Chakhai,

Jeev Mat Maar, Juva Mat Khelai,

Mat Par Tiya Lakh, Yahi Tero Tap Re,

Ghat Ghat Vyaapak Ram Jap Re !

"Ram that dwells in every heart, be he your constant remembrance. Bear no ill will towards any, and speak no falsewood. Pilfer not what does not belong to you, and take no intoxicant. Take no life, nor gamble. Do not cast eye on women. This alone will be your true austerity. Let Ram that abides in all life, be your constant remembrance".

### **Ghat Ghat Vyaapak Ram Jap Re** !

**Applicable To All Universities**  All the above matters, discused so far, are applicable to all the Universities in the Country. Practical ways of carrying out these suggestions may depend on each University separately - there may be better improvements also. But the changes will be far better than

"Students Association" or other Unions to act in their way of operation (may be good or may be political leading to aggresive demands, strikes, damages etc ) **The Big Question is-- Why BHU or other Universities did not follow the Best of the East Policy framed by Pt. Madan Mohan Malaviya ji--a century back????**

Many other Hindi Quotations on Sanatan Dharma, by Pt. Malaviya are given in the end, as a **Part of the Appendix.**

*NOTE-- Universities can pick up different <u>practical activities</u> for their students, so that they get used to follow Sanatan Dharma as an additional Curriculum of the studies.*

# Chapter - 8

# DHARMA IN PRACTICE 

{{ I would like to humbly place a few flowers on Mahamana and to his worthy policy 'Best of East'. I would like to see that the principles of Sanatan Dharma, expressed in lectures or in writings, are put into practice from the early age of students--particularly in all colleges and all Universities. Administrative officials and the professors could think of many ways, which help the students to grasp the principles of Dharma, through practice and experience. Practical learning has more power to go deep into the mind and the nature of the youngsters, so that they become what Pt. Malaviya had expected -- **citizens of high character, probity and honour.**

However, this Pratical way of building the Character of students applies to all educational institutions and Universities all over the country, irrespective of the religion of students. Therefore, the principle of Sanatan Dharma can be easily practiced in many other institutions and Universities. It has to be stressed again that Sanatan Dharma does not teach any religious subject, but guides how to follow the positive way of living together with the feeling of Ekatva between all and by the practice of good ways to live with unity }}

## PRACTICAL LIFE STYLE To Suit Sanatan Dharma

<u>Begins with Objections--</u> The moment we talk of Spirituality or Sanatan Dharma, many students and even some professors raise their objection that students <u>can not spend time</u> and also they have no inclination for "religious" spirituality. Education in the present day Colleges

/ Universities is on the main curricular subjects (various materialistic subjects). Universities, to increase their popularity, are keen to add <u>extra-curricular actives</u> to train the students in different ways. Examples are--

1. Boy Scouts, 2. NCC-Army, Navy, Air, 3. Games-many types in Fields (Cricket, Hocky etc), 4. Gymnasium, 5. Swimming, 6. Running, Boxing etc 7. Indoor sports, 8. Music, Dance, Cultural Activities, etc as special items - other extra-curricular activites are encouraged,  so that they bring fame to the College/Universities by participation and winning in different kinds of activities after studies. In short, the Universities are inclined towards --

a) good curricular subjects which can get high jobs with high salary for their students,

b) more students get quick offers for further studies/jobs abroad,

c) both above offers increase their Progress and Prosperity which gradually or soon hit hard, like roaring waves, to badly damage the voyage or reverse the path away from the goal. These rash foreign waves would lead to gradual discard of our own **customs, culture and heritage**.

Now the question is--if so much of time, energy, money of students and time of trainees/teachers etc can be spent on above extra-curricular activities, why not spend some time for guiding the students to  increase their understanding and following Sanatan Dharma?

Here is a beginning for <u>"**Practical ways to follow Dharma**"</u>.

## PRACTICAL FIVE ACTIONS -- Follow Formulas--

**1. Ekatva** means a) non <u>differentiating behaviour</u> with others. In short, Ekatva leads to a) <u>welfare of all students</u> coming from all parts of the country to the University; such persons should be of b) <u>no harm or trouble to others;</u>  they should c) <u>**try and help others**</u> (*Paropakaara*). Ekatva has a much wider meaning in general; but those details are not taken here.

2. **How to Develop Ekatva--** Professors in charge of hostels have to put together different persons, who are from different places/states/languages/rich or poor family etc. Gradually, let them come to know each other and be of help to each other, if required.

3. **Practice & Get Used To Ekatva --** a) **Develop** Mutual understanding with friends in group or team, with few close friends, b) help close friends when necessary, known as Paropakara, c) work with enthusiasm for social or team activities as in a small community, d) forget not your unity with big class or college.

4. **How to Mingle Amidst Variety of Persons---** Wealth, Authority or Knowledge of students may create differences with other students. Any one of these three items are likely to make a person **egoistic, dominating and selfish**, with no inclination to help or care for needs/worries of other students near to him. It is for Guru or Professor to teach that all three are negligable or temporary in life; because, wealth and authority may or may not be knocked off in any moment or longer in life. Also he may teach that wealth and authority could be happily used for philanthropy (Paropakara) and knowledge could be used as a cool transfermation to less knowledgable others. Hostel stay is a good step for mutual understanding and friendliness over a period.

5. **Another Step to *Ekatva*** among students, from all parts of country, with different languages, customs etc, -- each college could have many exhibitions/activities (artistic, technical, musical etc) in small groups (from different states) during annual celebrations or during convocations. This will also enable others to understand the students, their customs and good points in other places. During initial stages there may be laughing or criticisism of the different cultures, but gradually they will get adjusted by appreciating some differences.

## BE SPIRITUAL

**Five Senses Are Let Free?--** it has been mentioned earlier -"Do not get caught up always with 5 Senses--Eye, Ear, Nose, Tongue and Touch" and "More the senses indulge to stick to their choice, the quicker is the break down from pleasure to reach sorrow".

1. Pt. Malaviya had strongly adviced hostel students for Satvik food (vegetarian only) and  no wine or drinks. There was not much attraction then towards daily cinema and TV to take the student deep into imagination of 'lust and passion' (like the poison of the snake!)

Today, number of choices for tickling the senses are innumerable (in the present world) for momentory happiness or enjoyments. All the senses feed the mind any time, fill it up, mix it badly, confuse actions,much against the planned goal of the students. Today, instead of following the old procedure of games and gymnasium, most of the students are keen on getting their senses fulfilled in a lazy way. When demands are not met to feed the senses, big disturbances, strikes and damages come up!!

2. **Pt. Malaviya** was keen that students should practice in gymnasium, in the play grounds or in the swimming pool during the evenings. But today many students have other places to spend evenings-- out of BHU gate, Library room in Hostels or loitering around inside the campus, few in Central Library for more of free chit chat with lady students -- few go to the play ground also!!

3. All this is due to more attraction and concentration on the worldly matters, keeping aside Spirituality as a minor issue for little bit of time only.

**Social Service** Apart from games, Social Service is one way of controlling the mind in a better way, without leaving the sensories loosly. Students in different groups (teams) in the University could visit the nearby **villages** (assigned to them) and take up 'Social Service' work in many ways. The visits could be few times a year for each group. This would help them to understand the problems of the poor, help them (poor, defcient, poor in health, no education etc) to the extent possible. This feeling hits the youngsters and their sensories to a good extent. The students try to make some more improvements with their changed nature to help others, care for their worries etc. Gradually, their ego and selfishness will reduce.

4.  Some groups could take up other different ways of service like- keeping the University/ hostel/ residential areas/hospitals to be clean. Their planned effort could help in preparing good projects for a) 'Fertilisers From Waste', b) giving help to maintain cleanliness in roads, gardens, residential areas etc---c) some work  by cleansing areas, and by monitoring the work undertaken by workers. This type of service would expand their positive thoughts and work instead of getting lost in uncontrolled sensories.

5. **'Community Service'** is another way to brighten the society to better days and an eye opener to the youngsters. This includes many group works like--suggesting, experimenting, convincing others and a) implementing many ways for cleaner hostels, campus roads, vehicle parkings, b) collection of waste material in baskets of each sales shop (avoiding the  throwing of waste on road side), c) keeping the temples and surroundings cleaner and holier (with no noise or sound or talks by visitors, except the sound of pooja and chantings) and finally changing their own way of living for the welfare of the society etc.

All such dedicated works (for the good of society, of poor or unhealthy) will divert the mind from own fulfillment of own sensories to thinking of good for others.

**Further Ten Points (Look at the Practical Points)** these acts may look like a part of petty wordly matters and not the spiritual thoughts.

**Practical View** 1. --But gradually they teach us (and other people) about-  a) physical cleanliness, b) helping the society (*Paropakaara*), c) good and clean in all matters of life. In the long run, all these physical <u>clean habits should enable</u> to consider a) good work as sweet prasad from temple, b) consider a beauty around as your own sister, c) your minor help to others as a beginning to <u>help the men in small communities.</u>

**Practical View** As students become elder, they are likely to give importance to the town/city, the state and also the country of much bigger problems. In short, if <u>these small exercises are continued in many many universities, there would be a broader thinking to develop major changes in the State and the Country,</u> at least by a portion of the trained students. As more and more youngsters look at the problems cum solutions in small communities, (and as they grow up) they (at least 30%) would give importance to problems of the country. Finally their <u>improved patriotism</u> leads to our **country's major asset** (lost during the foreign rules and our poverty) **of spirituality to maintain our culture, customs and heritage---all become again important for enhancing patriotisom.**

2. <u>**Wealth, Authority, Knowledge**</u> <u>cannot be taken as the aim of life</u>. -Two points are important

--    Effort for Spiritual achievement should be there (even if it is for next birth)

--    Practice of Dharma to be initiated early (for a good /holy birth next time). Dharma expands from lovely home to good friendship, united community, positively activated state and a country filled with patriots.

3. **Practical View-- <u>Effort for Spiritual Achievement</u>**-- From the time of student days, they should be given goodinformation (and students should not decline saying they are not interested).  about--<u>idea of our Customs, Culture and Heritage (all based on Sanatana Dharma).</u>

They should be highlighted in a number of ways (to reach students & people), like- dramas, essay competitions by students; and speeches by experts on such subjects and their importance to be followed in future also. All these could be held in different Departments (on different days) so that interaction can be possible with students. Explanation of <u>Customs, Culture and Heritage</u>, their importance, the reasons for continuing them without fail, their connection with spirituality etc are to be given to the students. Explanations should be more important than the glorification of any custom.

**Practical View** Colleges were earlier united spiritually during special holy days. Gradually holy days have been split into cinema like glorious festivals instead of spiritual affairs. Now, it is essential to select few important customs to be repeated every year by students with more emphasis on subject rather than on the "show off" at heavy expenditure. The importance of our customs, meanings of celebrations of Rama Navami, Krishna Jayanti, Durga Pooja, Holi, Kumbh Mela and others are not mere grand celebrations to show off, they are graceful celebrations of many values to be appreciated and reminded every year to all. Most of them, including Holi, Kumbh Mela, Ganga Sagar Mela etc, are for every one in the colleges.

4. <u>**Practice of Dharma**</u> -- It is also essential to keep the students enlightened spiritually by certain important subjects (good under Best of The East). These include **Bhagavad Gita** classes (about 25 classes a year for 2 yrs); great saints of the past (6 in a year), great patriots of country (10 per year). These subjects for the students could be covered in their first two or three years of study.

5. **Practical View** <u>**Active & Positive**</u> --Dharma is following a set of rules in a particular way at particular timings. Other practical ways to ensure that students are kept active in many positive ways are ----(Each student could chose any one of the

following activities--

Boy Scout, NCC, Yoga Practice, Swimming, and any Sports Game (with all sportive ways, not with unsporting and fightings as seen among enemies).

No student should stay back in hostels for more than half an hour in a day (evenings), spending time for reading News Papers, Magazines, TV, Gossips, Loitering in the campus or out of campus  etc. Long exposure to fresh News Papers, Magzines, TV etc are more like loose talks and unwanted discussions. In evenings, they should be busy in any of the physical games for at least one hour a day.

6. **Practical View- Our Independence** Day or Republic Day should be a Day of Patriotism, which should be a part of the study from younger days. Learning to include how our country lost to invaders (from 10th Century), and how our people should regain patriotism --**should be a part of the teachings in every school-- to be taken care of by professors.** Just a flag hoisting and sweets distribution would not teach Patriotism.

7. **Political Splits**- When unity is very important, it is also essential that the Universities <u>donot allow political type of splits inside the University</u> (as it happened earlier in country's History). Political splits lead us away from spiritual sanctity and the splits get involved in fights that harm the University. The splits are then symbolised in a series of **lies, greed, steal fight (for power, capture, fights), complaints etc--even among students.**

8. **Lust for Worldly Matters** extends in different ways-- www (wealth, women and wine), high position, revenge for splits or fights or the power. In that fire of lust, even ladies are treated (not as sisters or mothers during splits, but) as targets to meet the Lust of a King or Beggar, as Market Stuff for sale, as Gadgets for Conversion into their Party or Religion ! For this reason, students (in their age) should be away from the practice

of playing with these three www, even temporarily. Satvik food as settled in BHU hostels by Pt. Malviya was a right way for carrying out this solution.

9. <u>**Three Sins**</u>--more types of sins come out--in some other cases-

a). some would be ready to do any work of sins with a bad purpose and a definite aim--ie, when one aspires/wishes for happiness; in order not to get into sorrow and when there is no effort to do good works the man commits any sin.

b).  Person is unable to decide what is good work and what is not by oneself; he leads to anarchy. One's thoughts  may be different from others. Therefore to think over and come to a good/correct solution without causing sin, there has to be a basis of Shaastras.

c). There are ten types of sins that get into the mind about other's wealth and posession; think and talk about doing harm to others; think of bad lust to satisfy the body in unwanted ways etc.,

10. **Practical View-- <u>Orientation</u> to New Students/Teaching Staff**

a) **Before** an  admission is given to any student, the Rules-Regulations-Serious dismissals for wrong doings, etc are to be signed by the <u>student and the parents</u>, about their agreement.

b) It is absolutely essential to have an **Orientation Program** in each College/Departments, when the new students get entry in the University. The present system of Orientation (in many Departments) involves in getting an expert in the particular 'high subject' to speak to the freshers. An youngster of 15/16 years can not understand the subject matter, much before their subjects are taught in the class.

c) Orientation should be an introduction of the University and Pt. Malaviya's great attempt to get the University with all the difficulty.

Objectives of BHU, the Departments, the teaching staff and the Dean, the do's and dont's by the students, rules and regulations in the Department and in the Hostel could be informed. What is allowed or not allowed in the campus etc and all such subjects also to be informed.

May our university teach students-properly-- Students Not to say lies, Not to steal anything, Not To Be Greedy For Every Thing Seen, and to treat All Ladies, (excepting the wife) as Your Mothers and not to commit sins that are not good for self and others.

**<u>Keep Up Our Identity</u>**--Greatness of our country is primarily based on Vedas, Upanishads, Samhitas, Puranas, Ramayana and Mahabharata. As metioned in earlier chapter, Vedas and Upanishads etc have imposed Dharma for prosperity of the country in many many ways like--a) **Positive**---acceptance of Almighty without arguements, not to be-little our Vedas etc, also divine help for protection of dharma, the art of Holistic living, hospitality, humanity, philosophy of social conduct and social service, duty, rule of law or code of conduct, healthy life, samskara, happiness and peace, sanctity of marriage and live as per Dharma Shaastra.

b) **Dharma has to spread**-- at home, with friends, in the community, in the state and in our own country. Dharma is vital for the progress and development of individual or mankind in its search for that goal of self -realization.

c) **Avoid Negatives - Add Positives in Behaviour** - All mentioned above are possible when there is no lie, no steeling, no ego, no pride, no arrogance, no selfishness, no show off, no false thoughts or false imaginations about too much of worldly affairs, no splits with others at home or in further steps outside.

Replace these Negatives with Positives like-good feelings, good talks, good help, good behaviour, good conduct, respect seniors, high character, probity and honour.

d) **Attachment Develops**--Worldly attachment leads to desire, when desire is not fulfilled it leads to anger, anger leads to loss of sence of good and bad, this leads to destruction of sound discretion and finally the loss of sound discretion leads to total discretion of man.

**Quick Escape**- When worldly affairs suddenly tickle any of the five sensories, learn to withdraw inside immediately like a turtle, take resort in temple, pray to Lord, remember your Guru's words, or beautiful sayings in Bhagavad Gita or Ram Charit Manas. The summary of action is -**"Protect Dharma and Dharma Protects You"**

e) **Practical View- Custom, Culture and Heritage--Custom** is one that is carried out usually in a simple manner, used for long time by practice, habituated as right or as a hall mark of old tradition. This may be old enough from long times as a part of correct Dharma in the family or particular community.

**Culture** is a state of civilization, over a long period, that has trained or refined the Mind in a particular way. Manusmriti says -"know Dharma to be that which is practicedby the learned, that lead a moral life, that are free from hatred and which is accepted by their hearts (conscience)." Thus, the role of mankind goes around in its search for that great goal--self realization.

**Heritage**-- that which is coming from early period---in the case of Sanatan Dharma, it is coming right from Vedic times.

One is supposed not to break or change the (age-old) Dharma by a new system or meaning.

**Practical Actions Possible --** when we look at few items like-

1) Five Tips to Remeber,  2) Five Beliefs, 3) Our Sins, 4) Control Five Senses, 5) Gear Upto Spirituality, 6) Physical Energy - Discipline - etc like Boys Scout, Swimming, Games, Gymnasium, Running, Boxing, Indoor Games etc. Each University can chose and give its own measure to its selected items.

( Note -- Before closing this presentation, I would like to give a few quotations connected with the **'Best of the East'** **values** -)

'People well versed in morals and firm in resolve, do not get distracted from the righteous path whether they are praised or abused, whether their wealth is gone or comes in, whether death comes calling today or waits for the turn of the century"--

That is the Righteous Path. Love for the good company of pious persons, liking for the good qualities in others, humility in front of teacher, interest in knowledge, devotion to Vishnu, love for one's wife,  fear about bad name of society, strength of self control, freedom from the company of the wicked--in who so ever these pure qualities reside, my obeisance to that great soul.

"Whatever is this country's vast thought process, whatever is the disciplined behaviour pattern, whatever is the exalted culture of this land filled with people of different religions, languages --Pt. Malaviyaji's personality was the best symbol of all these and the personified form of steadfast devotion and service" -- Dr. Vasudev Sharan Agarwal.

# "SANATAN DHARMA as AGE OLD SUGGESTIONS"

This is a small chapter, but important from the present day reactions to what most people, particularly youngsters, think Sanatan Dharma as "Age Old Suggestions" for improving the Values and behaviour of the students in this era!! The present youngsters of the universities, male or female, have not much touch, understanding or acceptance of the age old points of Dharma to be followed by all. In a way, they have strong feelings and approach for many issues or problems. For example, it is well known that Pt. Malaviyaji went to many houses in Banaras to persuade the parents to send their daughters to study in the University. The parents were afraid in many ways to admit their daughters in University--that the girls would be teased by students, that they would not feel free amidst a big group of male students, then about the food in hostels, the danger of playing games or free movements inside the university and participating in any functions etc. The old timers hesitated to send daughters to University and expressed their big problem of safety for two-four years and future problems for marriage. At that time, Pt. Malaviya ji was well known by everyone for his qualities and ability and he assured that the girls would be well taken care of. The parents were convinced by Pt. Malaviya's assurance and allowed their girls to join University.

But today, after hundred years of the University, things have changed, old thaughts have given place to much different and new way of thoughts and reasonings;

many views  have absolutely changed to opposite side etc. It is like an old father telling his son that as a boy he would walk few miles to the school etc; and immediately the young son would retort that the father was just wasting some hours, whereas he as a boy goes to school by bus and spends the balance time (wasted hours of father) for cricket or TV.  Even school students at young age, familiar in whatsapp calls etc, are intelligent enough to give different views of thought by the father or grand father!!  Similarly, in a factory or work place, the young person can be strong enough to talk or brave enough to argue his different view to the Manager. They may or may not easily be satisfied with a century old proposal in any matter.

Therefore, now a days it is not easy for the manager/professor to give a lecture on a fifty years or ten years old subject and convince the students or young workers. An approval also would be half hearted and may not proceed to work with full enthusiasm. Even if they accept it, or pretend to agree with it, the work may not go ahead smoothly and smartly as desired. Therefore, now a days, it would be good (by the professor) to briefly mention the problem or subject to students, and without expressing his further line of thinking, involve  the students on the problem to be faced.

It is better to start saying that--"I have a problem in this field and you youngsters, smart and shorp, may easily find out some good solution better than me. It would therefore be good if you can form your own separate groups to work on, discuss various possibilities, and in a week or two your group can come out with an opinion and solution of the problem.... You can also select your own group to work together ----similarly, other groups can also suggest their way of work.... ". This process means that you are **Involving Students** in the right way and to work on the project in their enthusiastic spirit.

When such a state of different groups come out by themselves, it would be worth giving them (in this subject) what others think as the "Old Frame of Sanatan Dharma" for their study or glance!! They would enthusiastically glance to see many charming and meaningful points of the work. The deeper they go, the better would be the meaning and brighter would be  the flash of solutions.  Brighter flash also is an indication of a good start of the engine!!

**Ekatva** (unity), -- a very important point in Sanatan Dharma, leads to social work meant to help the poor/ unhealthy/ uneducated people/ and dirty roads and other problems in the villages. Ekatva at home results in love, with neighbours in friendship, in own community with Unity, in the State or Country with patriotism. This is a wonderful episode worth following in all steps of life. **Cleanliness** in individual, in hostels, in roads, inside the University etc. These need not be once a year Program, garbage  can be used for continuous production of  fertiliser useful all over. These plans could be taken up with enthusiasm.

**Jealousy / Enmity** -- to be reduced/forgotten as per Sanatan Dharma, with a friend or neighbour or unknown person. Simple example to the present youngster is the current Cricket (or other sports) Tournaments. In earlier days winning or lossing a game was in true Sportsman spirit ! Today it is full of jealousy or enimity, with no Sportmanship, filled up with bad shouting (by player) and a worse dirty way of face towards the opponent, the moment one fellow is out-- a healthy game is turned into a nasty war, where enough richness is grabbed !!

**Discipline** --  to be maintained in all aspects of work, presence of group, prayer, music,  meetings etc,. Best example can be seen in Army, NCC training etc.

**Other Points** -- mentioned in previous pages as **Ten Points** could be looked into by the above process of "**Involving**

**Students**" in the right way and to work on the project in their enthusiastic spirit.

Also look at **Practical Actions Possible (as mentioned earlier)--**when we look at few items like-

1) Five Tips to Remeber,

2) Five Beliefs,

3) Our Sins,

4) Control Five Sensories,

5) Gear Upto Spirituality,

6) Physical Energy-Discipline- etc like Boys Scout, Swimming, Games, Gymnasium, Running, Boxing, Indoor Games etc. Each University can chose and give its own measure to its selected items.

This type of involving the students, their different plans, final solutions or final picture, their enthusiasm to see that their project would be successful  etc would become their own "Project to Work for Solution", not a Project taken up by the Department or University!!

# Chapter - 10

# SANATAN DHARMA IN PRACTICE 

So far we have seen 'Sanatan Dharma' in the way of a well written 'Theoretical Subject'. The details can be read or explained in speech to students. The matter expressed in speeches may be listened partly, or get confused by the students, remembered for a short time or take it only as an eulogy (a lavish praise) of the subject! It is therefore better that sayings of Sanatan Dharma are put into practice by a set of students guided by the Teachers. This practice should be taken more like other Extra-Curricular Activities in Games, Gymnasiums, Cultural Activities etc. Many groups of students may take up different problems to be tackled in different places. Few examples of 'Sanatan-Dharma' are shown below for practical usage by different groups. --

1. **Help to Needy Individuals** - (Help to bring them to right way) - Those who suffer from poverty, bad health, little education, no work etc.

2. **Help Weak Society** - Pardon-(Daya)-faulty Society, Show Pity-(Kshama)-to correct and improve them.

Group of ten students guided by Teacher can enter a poor village, talk with villagers, understand their problems, shortages, cleanliness, health problems, and join with them to make certain improvements in the society for their satisfaction after few visits.

3. **Improve Civic Sense** (Right Path shown by Youngsters is a prick to faulty Elders)

Group of students can work in different roads in towns, where both the sides are crowded by shops of sales items. Invariably, all waste/dirty items are thrown between the shop and the road-side. There is absolutely no check or prohibition and the road becomes dirty for cleaning in the morning. Group of students could take up the task and (with the help of Civic Officials) request the shop keepers to put all the waste in suitable containers within their premise --so that the waste can be lifted by the Civic workers in the next morning.

4. **Clean Up Residential Streets** - (Fertilisers from garbage is the simple part of <u>Ekatva</u>--encourage more)

In residential streets, the wastes are thrown all over the day in front of the houses. Student Groups (with the help of Civic Officials) can train / insist / ensure that house holders a) separate the types of waste, b) keep it inside the house till 7AM in the morning and c) allow civic cleaners to pick up all waste in the morning, d) Civic Dept. ensures to convert wet garbage into fertilisers etc. This will ensure that waste is put only in some baskets or boxes, instead of throwing on streets. These two jobs may look as "Dirty Jobs" for youngsters, but it would be a mild/good lesson to house-holders. Students group may continue the same method when there are shops in the streets. No need to feel bad for the good of all (as mentioned in Dharma). There is no happiness or peace without Dharma!! Dharma, the right way, is the back bone for the good of all residents. If not taken care of properly, it leads to daily Unhappiness due to  Adharma.

5. **Take Care of Scientific and Medical Waste** (Poisonous to Life and against Dharma)

Institutions and Hospitals carelessly (foolishly) allow the wastes to go down towards the river (seen by Author), even after knowing that these wastes are poisonous!!

6. **Indriya Nigraha** is equal or more important than the Cleanliness at home or outside!!

In the process of working and trying for positive changes (in others) in different places, students should not forget some points that may disturb their own Group or individually themselves. Simple clashes or disagreements with some person should be fully avoided by following many other points of Sanatan Dharma--

a) be away from selfishness,

b) discard looking down or laughing at others,

c) do not disgrace or disgust others, either by pride or fasion,

d) do not be-little and disgust/trouble others

e) do not get disinterested and move away from position,

f) do not be disillusioned and get away from mistaken belief,

g) do not discourage others with fear,

h) do not disregard or treat others with no importance,

i) do not waste or descredit their age-old customs-heritage,

j) involve in saintly work and treat all as same,

k) respect parents/elders, your God and your age-old belief.


7. **Indriya Nigraha for Self -- Patience for Others -**

A place with River and Temple can be improved by association with the small village/town. Group of Students can join with local people, investigate the reasons for pollution in the river, poor maintanence in temple, roads, house areas etc. They can discuss the reasons for the situation and join with them to work on different problems. Similarly you can avoid problems or dis-harmony with others by maintaining with them Patience, Respect, Faith, Belief, Help.

## 8. **Maintain Our Culture, Customs, Heritage -**

Go a few steps higher to activate the Pooja in temple, programs in festivals, re-institute the Cultural, Customs and continuation of Heritage.  These are gradually broken when one is unable to control his Indriya Nigraha, is mainly inclined to Progress and Prosperity, is more inclined to western ways of life and their association in many ways.Living in other countries affect the person to an extent, but the children (mostly) will be more accustomed from language to different activities.

More principles can be used for 'Dharma in Practice'

(NOTE--There are many books on the subject of Sanatan Dharma, other than the one written and explained in speeches about the real meaning. All the other books also narrate the idea of Sanatan Dharma, more or less in a similar meaning, detailed explanations are a bit less. However, the main parts of the other books are given here in th Appendix, so that any one can check for extra meaning or explanation. Brief portions of the books are shown here for any use. The books in Appendix are---

1. Sri Sri Bharathi Teertha MahaSwami Ji, Sringeri,

2. Sanatan Dharma, by 'Our Dharma 'Shri Dakshinamurthi Math, Varanasi.

3. 'Sanatan Dharma', in Bhagavad Gita.

4. 'Sanatan Dharma' Mrs. Annie Besant & Bhagavan Das.

5. Swami Vivekananda on 'Sanatan Dharma'.

6. "The Insights" By Pujya Mahuli Gopalacharya, Satyadhyana Vidyapeetha, Mumbai.

7. Hindi Quotations Of Pt. Malaviya on Sanatana Dharma.

Those Who Are Interested In More Details Or Clarifications, If Any, May Study The Portions Of The Books Shown below.

## 1. SRI SRI BHARATHI TEERTHA MAHASWAMI JI,

### JAGADGURU, DAKSHINAMNAYA SRI SHARADA PEETHAM, SRINGERI.

*(More explanations help in better understanding)

**Definitions To Understand 'Dharma'**

(Most of the portions are taken from the Kannada Book 'Sanatan Dharma-Part 1, which itself is entirely based on Jagadguru's Speeches over a number of days)

## 2. 'OUR DHARMA'- BOOK BY SHRI DAKSHINAMURTHI MATH, VARANASI.

**Life Too Must Follow A Rule**

Life too must follow a rule lest it stray and be lost in the desert of meaningless activity and noise, just as the waters should confine themselves to the <u>course in between the banks,</u>

and the <u>notes of the song conform to the rhythmic sequence</u>

Science also explains to us certain laws of Dharma. But it is a small section of Dharma confining itself to laws cognised (recognised, understood, experienced,) through the five senses of sight, smell, sound, touch and taste, whereas Dharma pertains also to things beyond the sense perception, to love, pleasure, pain and the innumerable experiences of truth. Acharya Shankara says (in his Gita Bhashya) :--Dharma of the Vedas is of two kinds characterised by **extrovertion** and **introvertion** and is the direct means to both—a) **worldly prosperity and b) supreme liberation** of all people. <u>Through extrovertion (**Pravritti**)</u> and active observance of Dharma in social life one <u>attains worldly prosperity</u>; and through <u>introvertion (**Nivritti**)</u> and renunciation, the <u>spiritual wealth</u> of Moksha. This double aspect and consequent double product of Dharma is an important factor. It is somewhat difficult for modern minds to understand that Dharma can show the path to a) **one who is rich and ambitious**, skilled and successful as well as to- b) another person at a different stage of life, desiring to give up all worldly possessions and devote himself to **spiritual practices** for the attainment of **peace through self-realisation**.

The hedonistic view (that only pleasure is important and required) of life is impossible and against Dharma, the nature of man.

**Science and Dharma--** You take a false step while coming down a flight of stairs; as a result you fall and are bruised. Why did you fall? Science readily answers, "Because you violated the law of gravitation". If further it is questioned, "Why did you get bruised now where as in many similar falls in the past you remained unhurt?" Science is silent. Here Dharma steps in and says "You must have violated your Dharma and hence had to suffer this pain". Similarly by lies, cheating, killing etc. you violate the internal Dharma (binding the universe) and suffer.

Must overcome many tendencies by practising truthfulness, straight-forwardness, non-violence etc. in all your actions. A stage comes when even these actions (lieing, cheating) are given up. <u>**Laws of renunciation** transcends through the laws of good and evil suits of actions</u>. This is the significance of **Pravritti Dharma merging into Nivritti Dharma** and the latter (**Nivritti**) leading beyond all Dharmas, beyond truth and untruth to utter peace.

Friendliness and love, trust and non violence, these are Dharma. Any act that springs from these feelings we can safely count as Dharma. When the awareness of the **world's unity** is strong then Dharma becomes easy and natural.

Dharma of extrovertion (Pravritti) must first be actively practised. It is the beginning, the first exercise for almost all of us. But as soon as we enter this field of action (in Pravritti), a thousand doubts and practical difficulties assail us---. Jealousy, hatred, suspicion, violence, cheating etc all are Adharma. The forces of adharma are turbulent and transitory; dharma is infinite patience and knows how to wait. But Atatatayis to be punished in time

Man is very sensitive to these. If he is physically hurt or materially deprived in any way he may take it easy, but on the point of what he **considers his honour he is upto anything**, even murder or suicide. So if any oné insults it, why should one be cross? And if another chooses to honour it, that too is quite deserving, there is nothing in it to get excited about, for the body, all the same, is a fine instrument for the supreme attainment of life's goal, Moksha.

# 3. SANATANA DHARMA
## BHAGAVAD GITA

Lord Sri Krishna has explained a number of positive points to Arjuna and they can be seen in many chapters of Gita. Few of them are mentioned here-- one should be free from the five sensory organs (indriya nigraha-abstinence) and keep praying to Me with diligence; with no animity with any animals (or living beings) ; be kind to all; do not have any ego-selfishness; treat sorrow or happiness in similar way.

In Shloka 12-8 of Gita -- Sri Krishna tells (to Arjuna)--concentrate your mind in Me only, make it firm, keep your wit (versatility) in the certainty of Me, then you will fully be with Me, there is no doubt.

Later in 12-12 of Gita--Sri Krishna says----knowledge is higher (better) than practice, <u>Dhyana is higher than knowledge; renunciation of the result is peace</u>. (**Dhyana** is focusing the (wide) knowledge to get the fruit of Karma).

Next- Sri Krishna gives a big explanation as to how one should be -- not hating others, friendly, kindly, not egoistic, keeping sorrow and happiness as equal, pardoning, always happy, -- and firm minded to be My devotee.

{ My Experience - I was finding it difficult to understand the above few shlokas and their meaning properly. After a long period, my humble mind reminded me of a strange experience in a Forest Guest House, where I had to stay all alone for a night, with only a cook cum assistant to help me. As a lonely person in a pitch dark forest, I had to spend an hour by engaging the cook to tell me about his life. His story is given here very briefly--- earlier he was a drunkard, meat eater, wife beater, quarrelling, neighbour, absentee cook-about to be neighbour, absentee cook-about to be kicked out of Guest House. He never bothered to go to any temple near by, leave aside the famous popular Kanwar Yatra to Baba Baidyanath Mandir in Deoghar, Jharkhand, Bihar. ----- To cut a long story short------ he once decided to go on a Kanwar Yatra carrying kaavdi full of Ganga Jal (from ) Sultan-Ganj to Baidyanath Mandir in Deoghar, 108 kms by walk. While doing Pooja of Shiv Linga by Ganga Jal, he did not pray for anything, except to say -'hey Shiva, enable me to come again next year also for your seva'. He had to purify himself (body and mind) for the whole year in order to go for the next year's yatra. And this continued for next 12 years (till then).  He became a completely changed person with his mind, customs, taking care of family-- turning him from a Tamasik person into a full Devotee (Bhakta)!!  }

Explanations of Vedas -- Upanishads -- Shaastras on Knowledge, Jnana, Dhyana, Renunciation, Karma, Indriya Nigraha etc are difficult to reach the mind or difficult to practice by the ordinary or Tamasic persons. Rajasic persons may or may not understand, but their reactions to follow or not is doubtable. For all such problems, mentioned in all possible ways, the major solution is to surrender fully as a devotee of the Lord. Bhakti with full faith on Him is the main solution.

# 4. SANATANA DHARMA
## BRIEF EXPLANATIONS BY
## Mrs. ANNIE BESANT & BHAGAVAN DAS

## Virtues of Students

1) **Body Strong, Healthy, Habits -**
Rising Early, Bathing, Eating Moderately, Plain Food, Plenty Of Exercise, Not Allowing Himself To -- Lye Down Luxuriously, Idle way.

2) **Youth- The Preparation Time of Life**--Industry, Obedience, Humility Service.

3) **Knowledge**--Absolutely Essential And **Useful.**

4) **Conduct and Humility**---Industrious Study; Obedience, Using The Experience Of His Elders, Humility Lifts Him Quickly.

5) **Chaste in Thought and Act**-- Celibate (Not Married) in Mind And Body, Guard His Thoughts, Think Not Impurity-Act Not Impurity, Think Not of Sex, Yield Not To Dreams.

6) **Study**-- Ever Engage In Study, In Services To His Teacher.

7) **Refrain From**---Wine, Meat, Perfumes, Garlands, Tasty Savoury Dishes and Women.

## Virtues to Draw Men Together

1) "Fearlessness, Cleanliness, Steadfastness In The Yoga Or Wisdom,

2) Alms-Giving, Self-Restraint, Sacrifice, Renunciation,

3) Study of the Shastras, Austerity and Straight Forwardness, Harmlessness,

4) Truthfulness, Absence of Wrath, Peacefulness, Absence of Crookedness,

5) Compassion to living beings, Mildness, Modesty, Absence of Fickleness,

Vigour, Forgiveness, Fortitude, Purity, Absence of Envy And Pride **Such virtues draw men together, and are based on the knowledge that all selves are one.**

## Morality-

1) - Object of Morality Is To Secure The Welfare Of All Beings,

2) Conduct of How To Live In **Harmony** With Others And Surroundings.

3) To Give Joy To Another Is Righteousness ; To Give Pain Is Sin.

4) Let Not Any Man Do Unto Another Any Act That He Wishes Not Be Done To Himself By Others,

5) Let Not Any One Do An Act That Injures Another, Nor Any That He Feels Shame To Do

6) Do Not Do To Another What Is Not Good For yrself.

**Morality** Has To Spread Between- The Members Of A Family; Between The Families That Make Up A Community; Between The Communities That Make Up A Nation; Between The Nations That Make Up Humanity; Between Humanity And The Other Inhabitants Of The Earth; Between The Inhabitants Of The Earth And Those Of Other Worlds Of The System.

**Aim is to bring** about universal happiness and welfare, by uniting the separated selves with each other and with the Supreme Self.

**Working together as a unity** for the good of the whole is one thing. The opposite creates all the troubles which make us unhappy, the quarrels between individuals, the poverty and starvation, the competition and the crushing of weak, the wars between nations and the countless evils round us, are all diseases of this great body,  due to the **parts of it getting out of order**, and working separately and competitively without a common object.

## Dharma

1) The Mark of Dharma is Achaara (good conduct)*

2) Achaara is the mark of the good. Achaara is higher than all teachings.

3) Achaara is Dharma born, and Dharma enhances life.

4) Achaara man attains life. By Achaara he attains fame.
5) Achaara is the highest Dharma, declared by the Shruti and the Smriti..

6) Dharma is declared for the well-being of all beings

7) **Student** Knows Dharma--when he is the friend of all beings ; who is intent on the welfare of all (in act, thought and speech) knowing it to be painful to himself.

8) Mutual Sacrifice, mutual service, promotes union
-all enjoined by the Sanatan Dharma.

9) "**Truthfulness, absence of theft, absence of anger, modesty, purity, intelligence, self-possession, self-control, restraint of the senses, learning this is declared to be the whole of dharma.**"

## Dharma.

That which inculates a set of **systemaized principles** --

a) for a healthy and beneficent life and

b) for a proper guidance to the man to step in the right path and to act properly,

c) to to be good for oneself and to others in relation.

In short , **Sanatan Dharma is the science of conduct to be followed all through so that good relation remains with others,who form our surroundings,**

## Satvic and Rajasic

**Saatvic** food increases life, energy, strength, health, joy, and cheerfulness,    non -volatile. Higher Evolution by predominance by Sattva--and it means harmony.

**Rajasic**-causing pain, depression, sickness,--bitter, acid, saline,over hot, punjent, dry and burning. The mind when wedded to indriyas, becomes Rajsick. When wedded to buddhi it becomes saattvic (p205)

**Rough & Tough** Shri Krishna speaks of **Divine and Asuric properties.**

1)    Divine --those which promote **union**, and as Asuric those which **promote separateness**.

2) Asuric--the qualities which drive man apart, promote divisions : Hypocrisy, Arrogance and Conceit,Wrath, Harshness and Unwisdom.

3) Truthfulness promotes union (Divine), while untruthfulness increases separateness.

4)    Truth is ever the dharma of the good. Truth is the Sanatana Dharma.

5)    Truth is the final way. Truth is dharma, Truthfulness, equality (impartiality )

6)    Self-control, Absence of envious emulation, forgiveness, modesty, endurance, absence of jealousy, charity, thoughtfulness, disinterested philanthropy, unceasing and compassionate harmlessness these are the main forms of Truth."

7)    Anger, lust, dejection, delusion, cynicism, wrongful activity, greed, envy, jealousy, irritated worry, sullen malice, scorn and fear these are vices and forms of untruth, are the **powerful enemies** of living creatures.

8) "Desire may not be quenched by enjoyment of its objects ; it only increases  manifold , as fire with libations of butter.

9) **Self-Control** " Forgiveness, self-possession, harmlessness, equability, truthfulness, straightforwardness, conquest ofsenses, skill, gentleness, modesty, restfulness, absence of scorn, absence of excitement, sweet speech, harmlessness, and absence  of jealousy of all these is the  source of Self Control".

10) **Avoid Bad company**; no company with people who are thinking unkind, or unclean, or other evil thoughts, or who are doing wrong actions impure, intemperate, gluttonous acts their feelings will work on us,  and will push us towards thinking and acting in a similar way.

# 5. SWAMI VIVEKANANDA 

In the ancient Bharat, the centre of life was more on intuitive and *Adhyatmik* subject and not mainly on politics. During the time of ruling by Mohammadens, Hindu movement was started in north India  so that the common man a) does not leave Hindu Dharma and b) does not get into that of the the Rulers. Because of this, every one got both the social and *Adhyatmik*  equality. Those who joined the sect of Ramananda, Kabir, Dadu, Chaitanya or Nanak --all of them agreed to teach that all human beings are same. **Their effort was to ensure that no one joins the Islamic** Dharma.

We keep our mind on the **worldly affairs**, but that alone is not enough, you have to keep attention on our **inner world** also. Today we are concentrating mainly on the outer world. That is because man is sticking more to outer world. <u>The desire to be happy makes him run after every material.</u> The external world of sensory (Indriyas) makes one a banter mind. Every sensory action is a momentary lust, happy or grief, wealth, authority, penniless, and even the life is so. There is nothing  to get the sensory happiness to continue for a long time.

Inner force or energy of Indians comes from Dharma; <u>whereas for the westerners</u> the energy is covered in the nice frame of politics (<u>in several ways from thuggery, deception, atrocity, day-light robbery, war and scheme to bleed others for one's need</u>).

Turning the man to Spirituality for the Bharatiya persons is the daily song, a whole life-time effort, the entire essence of life, the foundation of individuality, to be alive for this alone--Our country Bharat did not even slightly change its ideal, irrespective of who ruled the country--Moghul or the English.

# 6. SANATAN DHARMA "THE INSIGHTS"
## By PUJYA MAHULI GOPALACHARYA, SATYADHYANA VIDYAPEETHA, MUMBAI

## Negative Scenes and Positive Solutions

This is not just a story of BHU only. Most of the Universities in India have been stressing only for Progress and Prosperity, assuming that Dharma, Development of Character, Values etc are not part of the present Education system. Here are a number of examples to show how students abroad and at home also are getting far away from our Dharma, Customs, Culture, Heritage etc. The statements have been taken from some articles, but mainly from the book **"The Insights" (2011) by Pujya Mahuli Gopalacharya**, Satyadhyana Vidyapeetha, Mumbai. **Pujya Mahuli Gopalacharya** lived from 1909 till 1984, and it is likely that his writing might have been around 1955 and 1965--nearer to the start of big disturbances in BHU (1957 onwards). His observations are briefly mentioned here in simple points instead of full detail-----

**Sanatan Dharma**-supports and holds the people by a set of spiritual principles for ---- a) healthy and beneficient life, b) proper guidance to man to step in and act properly in the right path, c) good to himself and to others in harmonious relations (in the family, community, country or the whole world).

**Aim Of Education**- Real education should be a long process of **spiritual transformation** during which mind, heart and body are drilled and disciplined with great patience. The aim of education is not merely development of talents but to teach how to make the best of them. The poorest education that teaches self-control is better than the best that neglects it. Knowledge is the Supreme Good--Real education is the unfoldment of one's own soul. Try to co-ordinate their functions, harmonise their outcome and bring about all round development and integration of personality **Present Situation of Education--**(without its true system and spirit)-- --  the amount of ignorance in rudimentary matters is staggering; development of character with that of mind is lagging; driven away our joys, destroyed our peace and disorganised the joint family life; sown seeds of disunion; created dismay and disappointment. The age old ideals have gone; cultural values have paled into insignificance. Education that has nothing to do with 'that culture' is all stuff and nonsense. It makes people clever devils, lost to sin and shame. Students are not taught to realize that indiscipline precipitates the decline and fall of our nation. Descending to the level of brutes, they condemn what they do not understand and destroy all that they dislike. Though one is fired with a noble aim, he may not be a Visionary.

**What happens to Education--** also social customs are abhorred, elders are defied; universal revolt against God, religion and eternal values. More of these happen as students get into higher class-- First there is indifference to Values, next occasional falsehood, and then studied mendacity (untruthfulness) --progress on the road of foul play and dishonesty. Want of outward beauty of body, but not the **inward harmony in the mind.** Ladies or Gents take it as their freedom to stay together, fond of outing, enjoy company for food, drinks and even drugs, ladies refusing to marry unless their modern-western stylish lives are accepted by others  (far away from local customs and  making fun of old customs etc); the countless comforts and conveniences are given  prefernce to the old culture and customs! Society and individuals preferring modern civilisation in the place of our spiritual ways, culture and habits. These have led to disintegration of family, with old  parents living all alone. As long as the (western copy of) civilization goes hand in hand with our culture, it may positively lead to a global destruction. Rivarol said--"The most civilized people are as near to barbarism--an upward struggle of mankind"

**Religion is essential** to a full life; it is the surest refuge in the day of our trouble and the safest guide in times of prosperity. True religion is the foundation of society. An irreligious life is corrupt life. Our <u>material progress is spurious if it is there at the cost of religion.</u> Heart, intellect and body should be developed in co-ordination. If there is development of instinct only, the man would be a savage. If mind alone is cultivated, he would be inhuman. In a modern man refined thought and unrefined heart exist. Modern man , heavily loaded with labours and clogged with cares cannot think of God. The high and the low, the young and the old, the busy and the idle, the intelligent and the innocent alike shun acquaintance  with Vedas, Shaastras and the Puranas.--They have no time for such useless pursuits; or too high to give heed to any advice; the busy scorn scriptures; idle feel distressed; the intelligent say that they do not stand to gain any knowledge from the bundles of superstitions.

**Vedas and the Sanatan Dharma** teach us the best way of living, the sinless way of loving, the noblest way of suffering, most comfortable way of dying, the shortest way of reaching the final goal. Vedas are the ultimate decision in following Dharma, which does good for us. Therefore it is essential to follow the Karma imposed by the Shaastras. The most important rule to be followed by every one is "Satyam Vada Dharmam Chara". What is to be prohibited has to be decided by the Shaastras and not by our feeling or experience. The human life will be effective from the observance of Dharma. There are many Sanskrit shlokas saying what should be observed to make the life fruitful. Just a very few are mentioned here-- 'It is our duty to help others'; 'Helping others is a symbol of sacredness'; 'Develop the feeling that all are like myself'; 'Observe Dharma to get happinesss and to be away from sorrow'; 'One who feels/claims that what he is doing is right even after knowing his wrong action, that person is realy blind'.

There are five formulas to be observed as most imporatant --

1. Should not harm others;

2. Should not tell lies any time

3. Should not be greedy to have other's material--not steal,

4. Apart from own wife, treat every woman as your sister/mother

5. Should not be greedy for everything seen

To go up in the ladder of goodness/great in life, it is not simply by wealth, knowledge and authority, it is better to be a Dharmaatma for being a good birth and life in the next cycle.

**Advice to Students**-Your prime concern is to develop an integrated personality.Few points are--1. Not do anything which might deviate your attention from this purpose. Never deviate from the path of righteousness. 2. Be clean in in your body, speech, thoughts and actions. 3. Tenaciously preserve your Brahmacharya. 4. Avoid pleasures and perquisites; they can come only after the student days. 5. Never stop prayer to God. 6. Prostrate to your mother and father everyday, they are your visible Gods. 7. Do not take hasty decisions in life, decide only after consulting the elders, who are more experienced in life than you. 8. Keep your body fit by regular exercise. 9. Be grateful to society and parents who are helping you to grow.

10. Express your gratitude to them when you settle down in life after student days. 11. If you love-- your subject of study, your parents, your country, your tradition and your God, then all your love for trivialities will automatically go. Support this process by sticking to a self imposed regimen in study life.

<u>More Cautions -</u> . Our people who went abroad for studies have made great contributions to their family and country and are very prosperous. On an everage they are more prosperous than students of that country. One socialogist observed as follows---" The Indians who came here had **spiritual and familial values** and they worked hard to become Prosperous. But their children who are born and stay here, grow like the American/European children. By the next generation Indians will not have this superiority. There will be a definite change in the parents as well as the children". Prosperity would have changed the parents, changes in their speech, food, fasion and  life, including our country, our tradition, our customs, Heritage and our God and spirituality. The youngsters would have drastically changed, not knowing any of the above points.

**(Above matter taken from "Foundations of Dharma, by Pujya Sri Paramananda Bharati Swamiji)**

# 7. SANATAN DHARMA
## Pt. MADAN  MOHAN  MALAVIYA
## QUOTATIONS IN  HINDI

(**NOTE** -- Quotations given here  are only **a part of Pt. Malaviya's details of Sanatan Dharma.** It is worth while to use these quotations to ensure that we follow the rules of Sanatan Dharma  properly. Those  interested  may  plan  for  more activities  by   the  students. Part  of  these  quotations  were collected  by me earlier and a part selected from collection of Shri- Vasudev Sharan ji )

## धर्मसंस्थापना
### हिन्दी अनुवाद

परमेश्वर को प्रणाम कर, सब प्राणियों के उपकार के लिए, बुराई करने वालों को दबाने और दण्ड देने के लिए, धर्म संस्थापना के लिए, धर्म के अनुसार संगठन-मिलाप कर गाँव-गाँव में सभा करनी चाहिए। गाँव-गाँव में कथा बिठानी चाहिए। गाँव-गाँव में पाठशाला और अखाडा खोलना चाहिए। पर्व-पर्व पर मिलकर महोत्सव मानना चाहिए।

सब भाइयों को मिलकर, अनाथों की, विधवावों की, मन्दिरों की और गौ माता की रक्षा करनी चाहिए और इन सब कामों के लिए दान देना चाहिए।

स्त्रियों का सन्मान करना चाहिए।  दुखियों पर दया करनी चाहिए। उन जीवों को नहीं मरना चाहिए जो किसी पर चोट नहीं करते। मारना उनको चाहिए जो अत्याचारी हो; अर्थात जो स्त्रियों पर या किसी दूसरे के धन, धर्म या प्राण पर वार करते हों, या जो किसी के घर में आग लगाते हों। यदि ऐसे लोगों को मारे बिना, अपना या दूसरों का धर्म, प्राण या धन न बच सके तो उनको मारना धर्म है।

स्त्रियों को भी तथा पुरुषों को भी निडरपन, सच्चाई, चोरी न करना, ब्रह्मचर्य, धीरज और क्षमा अमृत के सामान सदा सेवन करना चाहिए।

इस बात को कभी न भूलना चाहिए कि भले कर्मों का फल भला और बुरे कर्मों का फल बुरा होता है; और कर्मों के अनुसार ही प्राणी को बार बार जन्म लेना पड़ता है, या मोक्ष मिलता है।

घट घट में बसने भगवान विष्णु का, सर्वव्यापी ईश्वर का, जिनके सामान दूसरा कोई नहीं, जो कि एक ही अद्वितीय है; अर्थात जिनके कारण कोई दूसरा नहीं और जो दुःख और पाप के हरनेवाले शिव स्वरुप है, जो सब पवित्र वस्तुवों से अधिक पवित्र, जो सब मङ्गल कर्मों के मङ्गल स्वरुप हैं, जो सब देवतावों के देवता हैं और जो समस्त संसार के आदि, सनातन, अजन्मा, अविनाशी पिता हैं, सदा सुमिरन करना चाहिए।

सनातनधर्मी, आर्यसमाजी, ब्रह्मसमाजी, सिक्ख, जैन और बौद्ध आदि, सब हिन्दुवों को चाहिए कि अपने-अपने विशेष धर्म का पालन करते हुए एक दूसरे के साथ प्रेम और आदर से बरते।

अपने विशवास में दृढ़ता, दूसरे की निन्दा का त्याग, मतभेद में ( चाहे वह धर्म सम्बन्दी हो या लोक सम्बन्दी ) सहनशीलता, और प्राणिमात्र से मित्रता रखनी चाहिए।

सुनो ! धर्म के सर्वस्व को और सुनकर इनके अनुसार आचरण करो ! जो काम अपने को बुरा या दुखदायी जान पड़े उसको दूसरे के साथ नहीं करना।

# धर्मसंस्थापना

मनुष्य को चाहिए कि जिस काम को वह नहीं चाहता है कि कोई दूसरा उसके साथ करे, उस काम को वह भी किसी दूसरे के प्रति न करे, क्योंकि वह जानता है कि यदि उसके साथ कोई ऐसी बात करता है, जो उसको प्रिय नहीं है, तो उसको कैसी पीड़ा पहुंचती है।

जो चाहता है कि मैं जीयूं , वह कैसे दूसरे का प्राण करने का मन करे? जो-जो मनुष्य अपने लिए चाहता है, वही-वही औरों के लिए भी सोचनी है।

मनुष्य को चाहिए कि न कोई किसी से डरे, न किसी को डर पहुंचाए। श्रीमद्भगवदगीता के उपदेश के अनुसार आर्य अर्थात श्रेष्ठ पुरुषों की वृत्ति में दृढ़ रहते हुए ऐसा जीवन जीवे जैसा सज्जन को जीना चाहिए।

हर एक को उचित है कि वह चाहे कि सब लोग सुखी रहें, सब निरोग रहें, सब का भला हो। कोई दुःख न पावे। प्राणियों के दुःख को दूर करने में

तत्पर यह दया बलवानों की शोभा है। धर्म के अनुसार चलने वालों को कभी इसका त्याग नहीं करना चाहिए।

देश की उन्नति के कामों में जो पारसी, मुसलमान, ईसाई, यहूदी देशभक्त हों उनके साथ मिलकर भी काम करना चाहिए।

यह भारतवर्ष जो हिन्दुस्तान के नाम से प्रसिद्ध है, बढ़ा पवित्र देश है। धन, धर्म और सुख का देने वाला यह देश सब देशों से उत्तम है।

कहते हैं कि देवता लोग यह गीत गाते हैं कि वे लोग धन्य हैं, जिनका जन्म इस भारत-भूमि में होता है जिसमें जन्म लेकर मनुष्य स्वर्ग का सुख और मोक्ष दोनों को पा सकता है।

यह हमारी मातृ-भूमि है, यह हमारी पितृ-भूमि है।  जो लोग सुजन्मा है, जिनके जीवन बहुत अच्छे हुए हैं : राम, कृष्ण, बुद्ध आदि; महापुरुषों के, आचारों के, ब्रह्मर्षियों और राजर्षियों के, गुरुओं के, धर्मवीरों के, शूरवीरों के, दानवीरों के, स्वतंत्रता के देशभक्तों के उज्जवल कामों की यह कर्म-भूमि है। इस देश में हमको परम भक्ति करना चाहिए और प्राणों से और धन से भी इसकी सेवा करनी चाहिए।

जिस धर्म में परमात्मा ने गुण और कर्म के विभाग से ब्राह्मण, क्षत्रिय, वैश्य, शूद्र - ये चार वर्ण उपजाए और जिसमें धर्म, अर्थ, काम और मोक्ष - इन चारों पुरुषार्थों के साधन में सहायक मनुष्य का जीवन पवित्र बनाने वाले ब्रह्मचर्य, गृहस्थ, वानप्रस्थ, और सन्यांस - ये चार आश्रम स्थापित हैं, सब धर्मों से उत्तम, इसी धर्म को हिन्दू धर्म कहते हैं। जो लोग सारे संसार का उपकार चाहते हैं उनको उचित है कि इस धर्म की रक्षा और इसका प्रचार करें।

धर्म ही सारे जगत की प्रतिष्ठा ( मूलाधार ) है।  संसार में प्रजा लोग धर्मशील पुरुष के पास पहुंचते हैं।  धर्म से पाप को दूर करते हैं। धर्म में सब प्रतिष्ठित है; अर्थात धर्म के मूलाधार पर सब स्थित है, इसलिए धर्म को सबसे बड़ा कहते हैं।

विद्या रूपं धनं शौर्यं  कुलीनत्वमरोगिता।
राज्यं स्वर्गश्च मोक्षश्च सर्वं धर्मादावाप्यते।।

विद्या, रूप, धन, शौर्य, वीरता, कुलीनता,आरोग्य, राज्य, स्वर्ग और मोक्ष - ये सब धर्म से प्राप्त होते हैं। सब से बड़ा उपकार जो किसी प्राणी का कोई कर

ये सब धर्म से ात होते ह। सब से बड़ा उपकार जो कसी ाणी का कोई कर सकता है, वह ये है कि उसको धर्म का ज्ञान करा दे, धर्म में उसकी श्रद्धा उत्पन्न कर दे अथवा दृढ़ कर दे। संसार में धर्म के ज्ञान के सामान दूसरा दान नहीं है। सनातन धर्म का सब मतों के अनुयायियों के उपकार के लिए है। इस सनातन धर्म का उत्तम वर्णन श्रीमद्भागवत के ७ वें स्कन्ध के ११ वें अध्याय से लेकर १५ वें अध्याय तक पाया जाता है। उसमें लिखा है कि –

## सत्यं दया तपः शौचं तितिक्षेक्षा शमो दमः।

सब धर्मों से उत्तम, इसी धर्म को हिन्दू धर्म कहते हैं। जो लोग सारे संसार का उपकार चाहते हैं उनको उचित है कि इस धर्म की रक्षा और इसका प्रचार करें।

यह धर्म बड़े बड़े गुणों का समूह है। दान, जीवमात्र पर दया, ब्रह्मचर्य, सत्य, दयालुता, धीरज और क्षमा इन गुणों का योग सनातन धर्म का सनातन मूल है। इन गुणों के कारण ही सनातन धर्म अन्य धर्मों से विशिष्ठ है।

धर्म ही सारे जगत की प्रतिष्ठा ( मूलाधार ) है। संसार में प्रजा लोग धर्मशील परुष के पास पहुंचते हैं। धर्म को पाप से दूर करते हैं। धर्म में सब प्रतिष्ठित है; अर्थात धर्म के मूलाधार पर सब स्थित है, इसलिए धर्म को सबसे बड़ा कहते हैं।

यह धर्म बड़े बड़े गुणों का समूह है। दान, प्राणिमात्र पर दया, ब्रह्मचर्य और इन्द्रियों को वश में रखना तथा सत्य का पालन, प्राणियों के दुःख में सहानुभूति, धीरज और क्षमा, ये सनातन धर्म के मूल है। ये धर्म ऐसे हैं कि संसार के सब धर्मों और सब सम्प्रदायों के अनुयायी इनका पालन कर इस लोक में सुख, शान्ति और सुयश तथा परलोक में उत्तम गति पा सकते हैं।

# CONCLUSION
## K. Chandramouli

Sri Shankaracharya and many other saints have explained clearly about the importance of Sanatan Dharma and the details of the do's and dont's for leading a good life. They have also been mostly followed by the Gurukulas or by the students strongly spiritual from the birth onwards. It was seen that even during the time of Pt. Malaviya, the situation was fairly alright to the principles. His preachings on the "Best of the East" were fruitfull to a good extent during his time; but, India gradually changed from a spiritually prominent country to the present mixed position, after the British rule. That was the time for our people here and abroad to be greatly influenced by the western cry of 'Progress and Prosperity'. But Pt. Malaviyaji was very particular about a good balance between 'Progress and Prosperity' and the 'Best of the East' Policy of Sanatan Dharma. This balance continued to an extent, and particularly in BHU alone, as was seen by the good charater of students who graduated from BHU till about the demise of Pt. Malaviyaji.

There after, the weakness in the balance was gradually visible in the frequent 'Student Disturbances' in BHU. I know about the student disturbances in 1957 when Dr. A.L. Mudliyar Committee was formed and the disturbances in 1969 when Mr Gajendra Gadkar Committee was formed to provide suitable suggestions. After that I have seen few bad disturbances during the Centenary Celebrations of BHU during 2015-2017. The worst fight among young students happened when a college bus was stopped and a student held the neck part of another student and dragged him down the bus. Other students also got down to see the problem. Both were about 18 or 19 yrs old, and one who was dragged down fell on the road. Immeditely, the first fellow hit him hard, many times, by pressing other boy's stomach by his leg ! No one stopped the fight and the villain continued at least for 5 or 6 times to hit hard by leg... I could not stop, nor I could see the horible scene. I came to know that it was a fight between two youngsters from two political parties!! They were all miserable to watch. This was due to the gradual weakening of our spiritual feelings of Dharma, our culture, customs and heritage. Attempts to improve the system, back to the original stage, were few and were not very useful. **"The Insights",** a book by Pujya Mahuli Gopalacharya (quoted earlier) has clearly shown how <u>**our country succumbed more to the western way of life**</u>, than to our own system of Sanatan Dharma, customs, culture etc. This explanation has been proved as correct by the frequent wild disturbances and problems that take place in many institutions all over the country.

Presently, the 'Best of the East' policy is mostly ignored. It does mean that all educational institutes are unaware of this Policy, based on Sanatan Dharma. Some are partly continuing with the old Gurukul Policy or else with the modernised Value Policy, assuming that Sanatan Dharma is based on 'Hindu religion!. The discription of Sanatan Dharma makes it clear that the education should again train the students to "live well for own character, for love in family, for friendship in community, for progress in state, for patriotism in country"--with no harm/harsh or bad ways of dealing with any group, with no unpleasant frequent disturbances in the Universities. I hope that all the Eductional Administrative Offices and Institutions will take more interest in **practically implementing** the Principles & Practice of 'Best of the East Policy' started by **Pt. Malaviyaji!!**

I am ready to give the first lot of "Students Orientation Classes" (Power Point Presentations) in all the 14-15 major Departments in BHU, provided the honourable VC and the Departmental Heads of BHU are ready to permit me or call me for it.

Apart from improving the future life of students,

**MAY OUR CITIZENS ENRICH THEIR PATRIOTISM FOR THE LOVE & STRENGTH OF THE COUNTRY!!**

**My Gratitude and Thanks to my Friends (from BHU and Bangalore) who encouraged me in bringing out this Book - Sri Sandeep Maini, Sri Pejawar Krishna Rao, Sri Trivikram B. Mallya, Sri MS Nagar, Sri Ram, Sri Manish Kothari, and finally Artist Sri SN Deshpande.**

**BEST OF THE OF EAST**
**For The Best Of All**
Brightened by 'Sanatan Dharma

"KNOW WELL & PRACTICE WELL
'TO SPREAD 'PIETY & PEACE'
FROM THE DUAL OF BESTS
BEST OF WEST & BEST OF EAST
( PRESENT OBJECTIVES OF B. H. U. TO BE SPREAD TO ALL
OTHER INSTITUTIONS )

Revised Edition: 2022

**Copyright © : K. Chandramouli,**
**Alumnus, BHU (1963)**
No 16, O.V.H. Road, Basavanagudi, Bangalore-560004.
Ph : 98452-79598    Email: kcmvcm@gmail.com

Book & Cover design : SN Deshpande        Book size : Demy 1/8